LANCASHIRE RAILWAYS
The History of Steam

MARK JONES

COUNTRYSIDE BOOKS
NEWBURY BERKSHIRE

First published 2012
© Mark Jones 2012

COUNTRYSIDE BOOKS
3 Catherine Road
Newbury, Berkshire

To view our complete range of books,
please visit us at
www.countrysidebooks.co.uk

ISBN 978 1 84674 298 9

Designed by Peter Davies, Nautilus Design
Produced through MRM Associates Ltd., Reading
Typeset by CJWT Solutions, St Helens
Printed by Berforts Information Press, Oxford

CONTENTS

MAP SHOWING THE ROUTE OF LANCASHIRE'S RAILWAYS

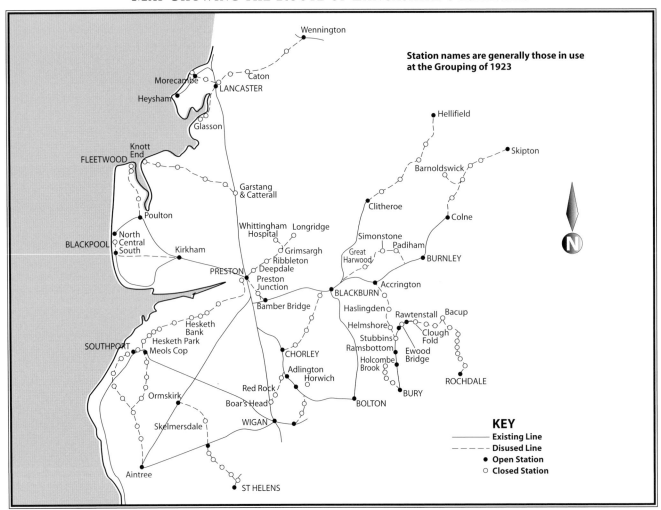

Wennington

Morecambe

Caton

Heysham

LANCASTER

Hellifield

Glasson

Skipton

Knott End

Barnoldswick

FLEETWOOD

Garstang & Catterall

Clitheroe

Colne

Poulton

Whittingham Hospital

Longridge

Simonstone

Padiham

BURNLEY

North

Grimsargh

BLACKPOOL Central

Ribbleton

Great Harwood

South

Deepdale

Kirkham

PRESTON

Preston Junction

BLACKBURN

Accrington

Bamber Bridge

Haslingden

Rawtenstall

Bacup

Hesketh Bank

Helmshore

Clough Fold

SOUTHPORT

Hesketh Park

Stubbins

Meols Cop

Ramsbottom

Ewood Bridge

CHORLEY

Holcombe Brook

ROCHDALE

Adlington

Horwich

BURY

Ormskirk

Red Rock

Boar's Head

BOLTON

Skelmersdale

WIGAN

Station names are generally those in use at the Grouping of 1923

N

Aintree

ST HELENS

KEY
— **Existing Line**
- - - **Disused Line**
● **Open Station**
○ **Closed Station**

IN THE BEGINNING

—■—

RAILWAYS HAVE EXISTED IN Lancashire for much longer than many people imagine, though little is known of what is thought to be the county's very first railway line – a primitive, wooden-railed, horse-drawn tram road at Prescot between St Helens and Liverpool. This line, owned by one Philip Layton, carried coal from a pit near Prescot Hall for about half a mile to Fall Lane, where one presumes a suitable road was available to take the materials to where they were needed. It had certainly opened by the early 1600s, but was possibly being worked as early as 1594, which would make it England's earliest documented surface railway. So, together with the Liverpool and Manchester Railway, which we will trace the history of shortly, there is no doubt about the county's pioneering role.

Why were railways necessary? Many sources detail the inadequacy of 17th- and 18th-century roads: narrow, muddy, deeply rutted, and with the ever present danger of musket-wielding highwaymen. These tracks could only be negotiated by horses hauling waggons or by trains of packhorses. So the first alternative was to use our rivers. During the late 17th century, Thomas Patten, a Lancashire businessman and merchant, was trading along the River Mersey between Liverpool and Warrington. In order to improve access for his barges to a quay just below Warrington, he cleared some obstructions in the river; the first recorded such 'improvement'. In a letter dated January 1677 Patten remarked that it would be an advantage to make the rivers Mersey and Irwell both navigable to Manchester. Around the same time, a quay was operating on the River Lune at Lancaster but, in 1779, due to silting and other difficulties, the Lancaster Port Commission decided to build a dock at Glasson. However, it was not until 1816 that Lancaster was linked to Glasson by a canal branch from the Lancaster Canal at Galgate.

The use of rivers as a means of transport had two main disadvantages. Firstly, they were narrow, tidal and greatly impeded by shallows and mud banks. Secondly, there was a constant danger of flooding. Most times the rivers Mersey and Irwell flowed peacefully along their meandering courses but this was not always the case. Whenever there was very heavy rainfall in the Pennine Hills, this quickly swelled the many streams that fed these rivers with vast amounts of water. The situation was especially serious in Manchester and Salford where the River Irwell narrows and its banks were crowded with mills, factories and wharfs. These natural and man-made constrictions caused the water level in the river to rise rapidly, creating flooding, havoc and panic. Records from as long ago as 1616 show that this happened frequently. So river 'navigations' were constructed and, though long lasting, achieved little in the way of profitability due to the cost of the constant high levels of maintenance required to keep them open, safe and free from obstruction.

A better option was to build a completely artificial waterway, a canal. One of the first of these new canals was the Sankey Brook Navigation which opened in 1757, linking the coalfields around St Helens with the city of Liverpool and the River Mersey. It was originally intended to straighten the existing brook; however it proved much more practical to build a man-made cut running beside it. The construction of more canals followed, particularly as the price of coal supplied through them significantly undercut the opposition. The Bridgewater Canal, linking Runcorn, Leigh and Manchester, was completed in 1761. This involved the construction of an aqueduct over the River Irwell – the first of its kind. This aqueduct was unfortunately destroyed in the 1890s when it was forced to make way for the construction of the Manchester Ship Canal.

But, as the development of bigger and bigger industrial sites took place, the demands on the transport infrastructure serving them started to become difficult to manage. For example, by 1786, the huge Ravenhead Plate Glass factory and its associated smelting works in St Helens were consuming well over 700 tons of coal per week between them. With these demands, the limitations of the canals as a reliable mode of transport were gradually becoming clear. Delays in traffic were frequent, with canals frozen up and impassable for long periods in the winter months when supplies were most needed. Conversely, water shortages during prolonged periods of dry weather could also shut down stretches of canal (and, of course, both these can still cause problems to this day). There was also much dissatisfaction with the standard of canal maintenance, with water leaking away at locks, and landslips

on embankments and cuttings not being hastily made good.

The other option was horse-drawn rail transport. One of the best known in Lancashire was the Walton Summit Plateway, known locally as the 'old tram road', which was built as a temporary measure to link two sections of the Lancaster Canal and included a bridge over the River Ribble, just south of Preston. But no aqueduct was ever built across the Ribble and the two parts of the canal which it linked remained forever separate. Construction of the plateway took three years before opening in 1795.

The 5-mile-long tram road comprised a double-track, 4 ft 3 in gauge plateway, except for a short section of single track through a tunnel under Fishergate in Preston, just south of the canal basin. The iron rails were 'L'-shaped in section and were spiked to large limestone blocks; the wheels on the waggons were not flanged and were kept on the track by the vertical section of the rails. As was common on early 'railway' systems, the waggons could be privately owned by the hauliers themselves (known locally as 'halers') who paid the company a toll to use the tram road. The last haler to work the tram road, John Procter, apparently walked the 10-mile return journey twice a day for 32 years; implying that he walked or rode an amazing 200,000 miles during his career on the tram road.

In 1813, estimates were prepared to replace the tramroad with a canal, including an aqueduct but the cost of £160,000 was too much for the company at the time. In 1837 the new Bolton & Preston Railway leased the tramroad as a potential alternative route into Preston that avoided the rival North Union Railway. However, a merger was concluded between the two parties before this proved necessary. This created a railhead for Wigan coal in Preston and removed the *raison d'être* of the tram road, which had finally closed by 1879.

So let us now return to the story of steam. Liverpool was becoming a port of huge importance, much to the disdain of inland Manchester. Rum and sugar from the West Indies, together with cotton and tobacco were coming in. Less worthy was the trade in African slaves until the abolition of such activities in 1807.

Heading out was salt from Cheshire, cotton goods and iron products, as well as the ubiquitous coal and stone traffic. Between 1800 and 1825 the population of Liverpool more than doubled, from 60,000 to 135,000. Manchester and adjoining Salford enjoyed similar expansion, bringing with it huge strains on housing and public health. This economic and social explosion was further supported by large numbers of military men returning from the Napoleonic War, all looking for work.

Around this time steam power was being developed

■ *The former horse-drawn tramway at Walton Summit, near Preston – now a delightful footpath.* (Author) ■

elsewhere, Trevithick in Cornwall and Wales; and Stephenson in the north-east amongst others was making significant progress with design and efficiency. The major sticking point was not the locomotive, though; it was the engine being too heavy for the rails that supported it. Nevertheless, the first

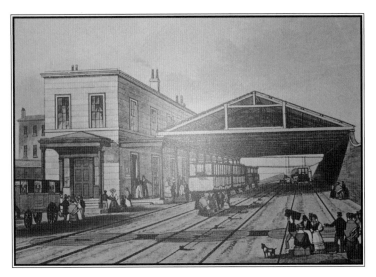

■ *An 1830s' Liverpool & Manchester Railway postcard.*
(Ian Edwards Collection) ■

proposals for a railway between Liverpool and Manchester, around 1800, were for a horse-drawn line.

Soon afterwards, one Thomas Gray set out a grand idea of a network of 'iron railways' throughout Britain and was certainly aware of the possibilities, if not the practicalities, of steam traction. By 1821 William James, another railway promoter, was ready to discuss with merchants and traders plans for a proposed railway between the two cities. James had visited Stephenson in the north-east, seen his locomotives in action at Killingworth and was impressed by their power and potential. Later, however, he fell out with Stephenson and

ended up in jail due to 'financial difficulties'. One of these merchants, James Sanders, was convinced of the potential benefits of the railway and was becoming impatient with the lack of progress. Eventually he was to push forward the formation of the Liverpool & Manchester Railway Company, chaired by Charles Lawrence, then Mayor of Liverpool. George Stephenson was appointed to oversee the entire project and in June 1824 he took up temporary residence in Liverpool.

Surveying and planning the route did not prove easy. The civil engineering issues we will explore in a later chapter, but Stephenson was faced with formidable opposition to the whole idea of a railway. The canal and navigation owners clearly had their own vested interests, but landowners such as Lord Derby and Lord Sefton were also firmly set against the railway passing across their territory. Determined to keep Stephenson from surveying their land, they set up fences and high barricades. Another of their tactics was to spread malicious rumours about the likelihood of steam locomotives exploding, although no decision about the form of traction to be used had been made at that stage.

Just as serious was the parliamentary opposition. As well as pointing out the unwelcome trespasses required for the survey, Stephenson's plans to build a huge viaduct over the Sankey Brook and the new canal attracted ridicule, and his ideas for crossing the marshy waste of Chat Moss even further derision. On 31st May 1825, a vote was taken in Parliament – the bill was lost. Although Stephenson was shattered by this defeat and a lesser man would have walked away (a civil engineer named Hugh Steele did take his own life shortly afterwards),

Stephenson determined to fight on. However, the company, resolving to get its line through at all costs, dismissed Stephenson a few weeks later, appointing Charles Vignoles who, though aged only thirty-two, had already made his name carrying out surveys in America. Crucially, Vignoles managed to get Robert Bradshaw, the man in charge of the Bridgewater Navigation Trust, to withdraw his opposition and indeed offer his support. Suitably reinvigorated, the company, now supported by local MP William Huskisson, who was sadly later to be killed in the first fatal accident involving a steam locomotive, put forward a second bill and this time with success. The Liverpool & Manchester Railway was ready to go.

Having impressed with his civil engineering talents, if not his parliamentary debating skills, George Stephenson was re-appointed as chief engineer on 3rd July 1826. So, together with Vignoles – though the two men soon argued and Vignoles resigned the following year – they began to stake out the route. Although some committee members continued to believe that fixed engines would be needed, as locomotives

■ *A contemporary print of Liverpool Road station in Manchester.* (Ian Edwards Collection) ■

might still be too heavy for the track and lack adequate power, the committee made a decision to seek motive power. It was at this point that a prize of £500 was offered (curiously for the 'most improved' rather than the 'best' engine) and trials were to take place at Rainhill in October 1829. The age of steam was about to begin.

THE EARLY DAYS

■ *A painting of the skew bridge at Rainhill by the artist T. T. Bury.*
(Ian Edwards Collection) ■

SO LET US RETURN TO **RAINHILL.** This stretch of the railway was very level for a mile or so and therefore a perfect site for the start of the trials. The trials attracted thousands of spectators, crowding onto specially-erected grandstands to watch the spectacle, but very few of them could have realised the significance of the drama unfolding before them. Three of the most eminent engineers of the day – Messrs Wood, Rastrick and Kennedy – were appointed as judges. Nicholas Wood was the Chief Engineer at Kinningworth Colliery, where he had been connected with locomotive work for some fifteen years whilst John Urpeth Rastrick, previously employed by the Board in the initial research activity, was a partner in Foster, Rastrick & Co., who had an engine building works at Stourbridge. John Kennedy had worked with spinning machinery, whilst his brother was later involved in building locomotives as a partner in Liverpool's Bury and Curtis firm. The reports of Wood and Rastrick, however, suggest that Kennedy's role in the trials was very small.

Cycloped was the first to drop out of the competition. This bizarre 'locomotive' used a horse walking on a drive belt for power and was withdrawn after an accident caused the horse to burst through the floor of the engine. Next to retire was *Perseverance*. Damaged en route to the competition, its

constructor Timothy Burstall of Leith in Scotland spent five days repairing it. When it failed to reach the required 10 miles per hour on its first tests the next day, it was withdrawn from the trial. It was granted a £25 consolation prize.

Sans Pareil nearly completed the trials; it performed very well but had a strange rolling gait due to its vertical cylinders. The 'blast' from the blast pipe was builder Timothy Hackworth's trademark style, in fact so strong that most of the coke was expelled out of the chimney unburnt; and it was this, more than its antiquated design, that caused its abysmal fuel

■ Cycloped *was a bit of a non-starter!* (Ian Edwards Collection) ■

economy. It was pulled out of the competition after completing eight trips due to cracking a cylinder; the thickness for the cylinder walls was meant to be 1¾ inches, but at the point of failure it was found to be just a wholly inadequate ⅝ inch. Despite the failure it was purchased by the Liverpool & Manchester, where it served for two years before being leased to the Bolton and Leigh Railway.

The last drop-out was *Novelty*. In complete contrast to *Cycloped*, it was cutting-edge technology for 1829, lighter and considerably faster than the other locomotives in the competition. It was accordingly the crowd favourite. Reaching a then astonishing 28 miles per hour on the first day of competition, it later suffered some damage to a boiler pipe which could not be fixed properly on site in the time allotted. Nevertheless, it continued its run on the next day but, upon reaching 15 mph, the pipe gave way again and damaged the engine severely enough that it had to drop out.

So, the *Rocket*, driven during the trials by Jon Dewerance who, in 1839, became Locomotive Superintendent of the L&MR, was the only locomotive to complete the trials. It averaged 12 miles per hour, achieving a top speed of 30 miles per hour hauling 13 tons, and was declared the winner of the £500 prize. The Stephensons were accordingly given the contract to produce locomotives for the Liverpool & Manchester Railway (L&MR).

■ *A working replica of* Sans Pareil *which is now on display at the Shildon Locomotion Museum, County Durham.* (Author) ■

■ *A replica of* Rocket, *on display at the National Railway Museum, York.* (Author) ■

of Kirkhouse for use on a railway near Brampton in Cumbria to haul heavy coal trains up gradients, its limitations became clear. *Rocket* was soon withdrawn from service, eventually finding a permanent home at the Science Museum in London. However, the Liverpool & Manchester were sufficiently impressed to order four similar but slightly more powerful engines known as the *Meteor* class and, as traffic increased, a growing collection of ever better-designed engines arrived.

The first operators of passenger railway services had very little previous experience to guide them as they planned their operations. At first, trains stopped at level crossings where the gatekeeper issued tickets to passengers; and sometimes a room in the gatekeeper's cottage was available as a shelter whilst the passengers waited to board the train. Only in 1841 were platforms and name-boards added to stations, so people knew where they were. Many of the stations consisted of little more than a basic house with no actual platform. In other cases, the company went as far as to cater for individual

In hindsight it is clear that *Rocket* was specially built for the specific task of the trials – this being to pull a limited load along a level track – one requiring little tractive effort. Indeed, after *Rocket* was sold for £300 in 1836 to one James Thompson

families by arranging for trains to stop at lineside isolated farmhouses in areas such as Chat Moss. Both the original terminus stations only had a single platform, which quickly proved insufficient; Crown Street passenger terminus being closed on 15th August 1836 and replaced by a new terminus at Lime Street, much closer to the city centre. It may be noted that other early stations in Lancashire proved equally ineffective. Tickets were sold in pubs, notably at the Three Pigeons at Dallam, Warrington and the Plough at Grimsargh on the Longridge Branch. Lancaster's first station, at Penny Street – which still survives – was also quickly replaced by the current station below the castle.

■ *The old dock at Widnes. This was the first purpose-built rail-connected dock anywhere in the world.* (Author) ■

But the early and noted success of the L&MR did lead to a number of other local lines springing up which rapidly formed a 'network'; one being the St Helens (or St Helens & Runcorn Gap) Railway. The St Helens Railway was actually under construction before George Stephenson had completed the L&MR and a bridge, west of St Helens Junction station and now much modified, is the earliest 'rail over rail' bridge anywhere in Britain. Widnes, then known as 'Runcorn Gap', was the southern terminus of the line which ran almost due south from St Helens. The line opened on 21st February 1833,

with the primary purpose being the movement of coal to the Mersey for transhipment to barges or small sailing vessels known as Mersey Flats that would then go down river to Liverpool. Extensive dock facilities were laid out at Runcorn Gap with rail connections, the world's first direct rail to ship facility of its kind.

The people of St Helens lobbied the St Helens and Runcorn Gap Railway Company for a passenger service to Runcorn Gap and, in September 1833, the company hired two coaches from the LMR at £1 per coach per week and began a service. No specific passenger trains were run; instead the coaches were attached to coal trains. It was at this time that Runcorn Gap station opened. No pictures exist of it but early maps show the most basic of facilities. In 1838, over 26,000 passengers used the line but very little thought was given to them. The line did not even submit a timetable for the latterly famous, national *Bradshaw* publication which began in 1839. It had two steep inclines on its route, one just north of Runcorn Gap, where trains were hauled up by cable. There is a record of a passenger who arrived at Runcorn Gap station in the early 1840s to find the train gone. The station master apparently sold him a ticket and said 'If you rush along the line, you will easily catch it up'. Such was the quality of the service! From 1845 the line was doubled and the inclines eased. This meant a journey time of only 25 minutes from St Helens to Runcorn Gap but still passenger facilities and services did not improve much.

In 1845 the railway company amalgamated with the St Helens Canal to form the St Helens Canal & Railway Company and, on 1st July 1853, the St Helens Canal & Railway Company opened its line to Garston, with much better dock facilities and, on this occasion, more consideration was given to passengers. A new station opened, still termed Runcorn Gap rather than Widnes, but much closer to the town centre. The line through the site of the old Runcorn Gap station continued in use for goods services until the late 1960s when the lines were lifted. Just to the south of the station there had been a swing bridge which carried the line across the St Helens Canal to the old docks. The bridge survived until the early 1980s when it was replaced by a wooden footbridge and the whole area was laid out as a park.

As the railways developed, the Railway Department of the Board of Trade encouraged the process of standardisation, mainly with regard to safety systems and signals. By now, the railway companies were very powerful organisations. Parliament at the time was dominated not by party politics but by interest groups and the railways were amongst the most powerful of these. As a result, most of the Railway Department's rules were only applicable to lines and installations built after the rules were drawn up, and few changes were forced onto the existing companies – commercial and profit interests were the only considerations.

Signalling was a prime example. There was no signalling between Liverpool and Manchester at all at this time, in the manner we know today. The instruments were controlled by the railway company's signalmen at both ends of the block, not by telegraph clerks. This was a problem in that there were no means of communication between the various signal boxes along the line and information regarding the state of the rails, traffic, weather and other conditions could not be passed on. As the railways became busier and busier, accidents became more common and it was clear that something more failsafe and better equipped for the volume of traffic was urgently required. The *Civil Engineer & Architect's Journal* of 1857 picks up the story:

'Among the more recent improvements adopted by the London and North-Western Company for securing perfect safety of travelling over their line, has been the establishment of a "special train telegraph", with

signal stations every two miles. At each station a "policeman" is on duty night and day, in whose watch-box there is a telegraph dial with a single needle. By inclining the needle to the left hand, the person in charge gives notice to the next station that a train had passed on to the two miles of the road entrusted to his special care; while inclining it to the right hand would show that the train had passed off that portion of the line. There were in fact but two signals, "train on" and "train off", but as it might happen that an accident occurred upon the two miles of road between the telegraph stations, the guard and brakeman were instructed instantly to sever the "special train wire", which has the effect of placing the needle at each adjacent station in an upright position.'

Clearly such operators quickly became known as signalmen and the semaphore system that it made use of has only in recent times been replaced by coloured lights and, in places, radio communications.

So by 1870 the essential features of the railway industry – the basic network, organisational structure and traffic patterns – had been established. But maturity did not mean stagnation. From 1870 to 1914 there was a four-fold increase in passengers and a three-fold increase in freight. Route-mileage increased by 50%, capital by 150% and gross revenue by nearly 200%. In fact it can fairly be said that inland transport was essentially rail transport in the late 19th century, though this is not to ignore altogether the important role of short-distance, horse-drawn, road transport.

■ *Traditional semaphore signal on the East Lancashire Railway at Ramsbottom. (Author)* ■

Laying the Tracks

■

CIVIL ENGINEERS HAD THREE big challenges to overcome when building a railway: they needed to be able to build tunnels, construct viaducts and find a way to cross marshy, boggy terrain.

The latter problem was a key issue for the Liverpool & Manchester Railway as it had to cross Chat Moss, then a 4-mile stretch of swamp almost impossible for a man to set foot on, let alone build a heavy railway suitable for carrying hundreds of tons of train. The dangers quickly became clear. One early gang leader named John Dixon suddenly sank down to his knees then, as he panicked, he dropped further and further into the mud. Labourers close by somehow managed to find some timbers and haul him out, caked in filth, but poor Mr Dixon was traumatised and very reluctant to continue with his work on the moss. Nevertheless, work proceeded and George Stephenson was to tackle the task with a remarkable and revolutionary design.

First he drained the surrounding area as best he could by building drainage channels, then constructing what amounted to a 'floating formation'. One of the men on the site, Robert Standard, suggested a plan that would produce a firm but pliable track. Stephenson accepted Standard's idea of timber laid in herring-bone fashion. This was combined with moss, heather and brushwood hurdles which, for month after month, were pushed further and further into the murky depths of the moss until a bottom was touched 25 ft down and a relatively stable embankment was able to rise just above the surface of the bog. To this day the line has a lower speed limit than other main routes, and even a lightweight modern multiple unit will start to sway slightly from side to side if driven across at too high a speed.

One other interesting development came about as a result of the Chat Moss works. To reduce the static load, Stephenson

■ *An early train crossing Chat Moss.* (Ian Edwards Collection) ■

used wooden sleepers placed at right angles to the rails; these cross-ties had been ineffective on earlier horse-drawn lines as, unless they were completely buried under ballast or some another material, they would quickly become damaged by the hooves of the haulage horses. But these new sleepers proved far more satisfactory than the old stone blocks and, after conversion of the whole L&MR line in 1837, became the accepted method of securing the track as many more lines were built. Some of the L&MR's old stone sleeper blocks were actually sold and re-used on the Storeton Tramway, a very late horse-drawn route on the Wirral.

The Liverpool & Manchester Railway also built tunnels, but nothing quite as long as that constructed by the Lancashire & Yorkshire Railway (LYR) on their trans-Pennine route between Rochdale and Todmorden. Tunnels weren't quite such cutting edge pieces of civil engineering as 'floating tracks'. A number of long canal tunnels had already been built by then and what was probably Britain's first railway tunnel had opened in 1796, not too far away at Chapel Milton, near Chapel en le Frith in Derbyshire.

George Stephenson was the man involved again, contracted as engineer to the Summit Tunnel. This opened in 1841, was 2,885 yards in length and on a 1 in 330 gradient (which helped with drainage). Building such a tunnel was a huge task. First the geology had to be established whilst detailed ground analyses and probe drills were made. Rock crevices not only make digging more difficult, but a new tunnel can also experience sudden and uncontrollable infusions of water during construction, especially if the tunnel is deep below ground or built under water.

A tunnel dug through stone had to be excavated by means of perforation and dynamiting. The roof of the tunnel could only be left unsupported for a short time, as the tension readjustment after explosive use amongst small rocks could cause the stone to collapse. Therefore bolstering was needed very soon after excavation.

The earliest way to build a tunnel was to start digging from each end and meet somewhere in the middle. Although fine for short tunnels, this method was far too slow for any decent length so another technique involved the use of construction shafts and headings. A number of shafts were sunk, reasonable distances apart, along the alignment of the tunnel. These shafts were usually lined as far as the tunnel's roof level, and then continued downwards to below floor level, supported in timber. By digging down deeper than the floor, it meant that a sump could be formed to collect groundwater.

Once all the required shafts had been constructed, a series of small tunnels or 'heading' – usually in the region of 1.5 metres high by 1 metre wide – was driven between the shafts. These were created with timber supports and used to ensure that alignment and levels were correct through the tunnel. In straight bores, candle-pots were often lit at the base of each shaft as a quick way of revealing any discrepancies. When this stage was completed, excavation of the full bore could be started. So a tunnel, with four construction shafts, could have a maximum of ten gangs of navvies working simultaneously at ten faces – two gangs per shaft working both ways, and another at each end of the tunnel.

Stephenson was very proud of his tunnel, once stating that 'I will stake my character and my head if that tunnel were to

■ *Nineteenth-century navvies, relying on shovels and pickaxes to force their way through the rock.* (Ian Edwards Collection) ■

give way'. One hundred and forty-four years later, on Thursday 20th December 1984, his words were to prove prophetic. Very early that morning a fully-loaded tanker train became derailed; an axle on the fourth tanker of a thirteen-wagon train broke, causing the tanker to fall onto its side. The train was transporting over one million litres of four-star petrol. The fuel began escaping and was quickly ignited upon contact with the hot broken axle. The train crew saw flames dancing through the ballast and, realising disaster was underfoot, ran for one mile to safely escape at the southern end of the tunnel and raise the alarm. Fire crews from the Greater Manchester and West Yorkshire brigades were quickly in attendance. Fortuitously, both had participated in a joint training exercise for just such an event only one month before.

■ *The fire raging around the Summit Tunnel.* (Author's collection) ■

The emergency services were able to persuade the crew to return to the train, where they were able to drive the locomotive and the first three tankers out of the tunnel, thus removing a large amount of fuel from the scene and clearing the way for the fire fighters; an extraordinary act of bravery.

■ *The devastation inside the tunnel.* (Author's collection) ■

Meanwhile, crews began tackling the fire from both ends of the tunnel, and lowered hoses down some of the ventilation shafts.

Just after 9.30 am, pressure in one of the wagons rose to a point where its release valves popped open, allowing pressurised vapour to gush forth. This immediately ignited and the flames were forced by the tunnel wall to be deflected in both directions. The fire crews had to quickly retreat, and all were able to escape the tunnel before the first of a number of explosions. The petrol flooded along the tunnel floor, but now there was not enough oxygen to allow the fuel to burn readily. The needy combustibles found their way up two of the tunnel ventilation shafts in the form of superheated gas, where the gases ignited and became a spectacular column of fire which rose 150 ft into the air.

Despite the temperature in the tunnel reaching an estimated 2000°C, only the outer three of the six rings of brickwork in the tunnel were badly damaged – a remarkable tribute to Stephenson and all those responsible for its construction. To restore it, British Rail had to replace the track and electrical services, shore up the bases of vent shafts 8 and 9 and fill the two shafts with inert foam. After just eight months, train services resumed through the tunnel but not before the public were given a one-off opportunity to walk through it on 19th August 1985.

Last, but not least, let us consider viaducts. Although many people in the north-west will be more familiar with the even bigger structure just north of Stockport station, the longest and largest railway viaduct in Lancashire is situated at Whalley between Clitheroe and Blackburn. It was built between 1846 and 1850 to carry the Bolton, Blackburn, Clitheroe and West Yorkshire Railway nearly 70 ft above the River Calder for some three quarters of a mile.

Engineered by T.W. Flanagan, its size may be best conveyed by quoting some figures: over seven million bricks and 12,338 cubic metres of stone were used in construction. Three thousand metres of timber were used for the arch centring, temporary platforms and the permanent foundation piles. With no doubt some awareness of the crossing of Chat Moss, a raft was used to cross the river because of the risk of quicksand, with oak and larch beams laid to form part of the foundations.

Let us look at one of these figures in a little more detail. Seven million bricks – from where could such an amount possibly be found? The railway's answer was novel. It was decided to recruit its own brick makers. George Clarke, originally from Buckinghamshire, was appointed in 1841 to seek out a brick maker and he contracted one Thomas Hilton to carry out the mammoth task. Many of Hilton's bricks were made locally in Whalley itself, from clay taken from Hardle Common, close to the brick kilns which were set in what is now Riddings Lane. The bricks were taken down in wagons to the side of the line and drawn up in wheelbarrows by horses, with a pulley. A man at the top pulled the barrows on as they arrived; the barrow being let down by hooking the wheel. Clarke later moved to Rishton where he established major brickworks at Norden Mill. Later on he became a noted figure, responsible for building the Victoria Mill and establishing a Wesleyan chapel in the small town.

The viaduct, known locally as Whalley Arches, has always had problems with stability. On 6th October 1849, during construction, two of the finished 41 arches collapsed, with the loss of three lives. Then, in 1941, a serious crack was discovered in one of the arches over the river. The foundation of the column in the river had collapsed and the leg was literally hanging from the top. Only some of the original oak beams had stood the strain of the hundred years which had supported the towering arch above. Piles were drilled 40 ft down into a shelf of rock known as the Pendle Shelf. The column was underpinned and it now rests on the piles. The river bank and the two adjacent columns were supported in the same way. This work took almost three years to complete; in fact, nearly as long as it had taken to build the whole viaduct.

■ *Whalley viaduct under construction.* (Author's collection) ■

More recently, Network Rail engineers discovered that one of its 49 arches had begun to slip because some more of the wooden pilings had rotted. New steel pilings were inserted and the underneath of the arch was sprayed with concrete. The work took around nine months to complete. A spokesman said, 'It's not something that's serious enough that needs the line closing' and reassuringly added, 'Train services on the viaduct have a 45 mph limit and that's perfectly acceptable for the type of distortion there is in the viaduct'.

■ *Whalley viaduct is still carrying trains today.* (Glenn Morris) ■

THOSE WHO MADE IT HAPPEN

■

WE HAVE TOUCHED ON THE PIONEERS, those men who strode forward to plan, survey and think up ever more ingenious ways of getting a railway across our not always straightforward terrain. Let us now take a look at the men who were behind the building and running of it all.

First we must consider the navvies. By the mid 1850s, at the height of railway mania, there were some 250,000 navvies put to work around the country, laying thousands of miles of rail lines. Almost all the work was done without the use of machinery. Instead, the standard tools of the navvies were picks, shovels and a wheelbarrow.

Navvies generally lived in so-called shanty towns, erected by the rail line that they were building. Huts could accommodate twenty men who each paid 1½ pennies for a bed for the night. Those who slept on the floor paid less – five nights on the floor cost one penny. The navvies would sometimes also be transported to and from their place of work on what were usually known as 'paddy mails', leaving at about 5.30 each morning.

The men who built the quarry lines fared even worse. They worked in the open moorland with no safety equipment, using only hammers, picks, crow bars and sledge hammers to force the stone from the rock beds. It was often said that you would never see an overweight quarryman, and the hard physical labour ensured that was the case. The large pieces of rock, weighing from one to seven tons, would then be lifted by a steam crane to the work areas where they could be split again into manageable sizes and the banker masons could finally shape the sandstone to the correct measurements.

By the standards of the time, navvies were well paid. They could earn five shillings a day which compared very well with those who worked in the mills and factories. Because of these rates of pay, navvies were seen as expendable. They were easy to recruit and replace, and many lost their lives when carrying out more dangerous tasks such as tunnel construction. A widow might get £5 compensation if she was very lucky. The drinking habits of the navvies were well known and many towns feared the arrival of the navvies to their region. Navvies worked hard and they drank hard. 'Going on a randy' was navvy slang for going on a drinking spree that could last several days. Work on the rail line might stop and people in the towns feared for their safety. Only the taverns, many of which were owned by the railway companies, were happy about the high spending on alcohol.

If the railway builders were seen as itinerants, the people who staffed the railways were seen in a very different light. Late Victorian and Edwardian station masters were perceived as highly respected individuals, but in the case of station masters before 1870 these attributes are not necessarily applicable. Britain's pioneer station masters were a very mixed bag, to say the least. One such was Benjamin Baddeley, for

■ *The work of the navvies was, to put it mildly, very hard physical labouring. A good navvy could shift 20 tonnes of earth in a day.* (Bertram Baxter Collection) ■

■ *An unidentified photo of track workers.* (Glenn Morris Collection) ■

by then an essential piece of equipment. Some spent more time than they should have socializing in the pub, whilst others were uncomfortable managing staff or handling tickets and money.

But, in more recent times, railwaymen were pillars of their communities – even gangers or cleaners who might very well spend their whole working life at the same station doing the same job. Whatever their job, they took it seriously and with clear pride. Porters and platelayers, fitters and drivers all quickly acquired a common tradition of service, often in conflict with unnecessarily blunt central management.

Jobs did not always quite correspond to their titles, though. Engine cleaners, for example, didn't just clean engines, they were kept busy on a thousand and one other general shed duties. These included keeping the locomotive sand-hole fire burning to ensure the sand was kept free-running; going around the shed

several years stationmaster at Pennington near Leigh, who was actually an old soldier and who had fought at Waterloo. Many problems arose due to the lack of education and training. In the 1850s some had still not mastered the use of the telegraph,

ensuring that each loco had a pair of lamps; and also that they each had a full complement of fire irons, namely a paddle, a dart, and a pricker. In the winter the cleaner also had to maintain frost-fires, located in braziers adjacent to the water columns. These needed to be kept well-supplied with coal in order to prevent freezing of the water in the columns.

The most glamorous job was obviously that of the driver, but this was a distant dream for most aspiring railwaymen. Usually starting as a cleaner, the aim was to reach the next step up, that of fireman. If a cleaner passed a 'test' of competence, he could be called upon for firing duty; and after 313 days of firing (a year, less 52 rest days) he would be paid a fireman's wage whether he was cleaning or firing. Alongside the obvious need to keep the boiler stocked up, a fireman had to learn about coupling up to the passenger train, including ensuring the correct attachment for the vacuum brake pipe and, during the winter season, also the steam heating pipe. This was as much part of his job as his footplate duties.

■ *Staff posing at Haslingden station in early LMS days.* (Author's collection) ■

A similar system of promotion led to the appointment of driver, a highly sought-after post. There were sub grades that could be worked up to: the first stage was engine preparation and dispersal within the depot yard, then progress was made to shunting local freight, long-distance freight, local passenger

■ *Staff at Blackpool Central station in the 1930s. (Author's collection)* ■

could then be kept nicely warm on a tray above the firebox. It was possible, unofficially of course, to make a rather fine breakfast: eggs, bacon and mushrooms could all be fried on a shovel. First, the shovel was cleaned using high pressure water from the slacking pipe. After the shovel had been dried, fat was placed on the shovel, followed by the food and it was then shoved into the firebox. At such a temperature, a minute or so of frying time was sufficient!

Such frivolities were not part of the wartime driver's lifestyle, though. Often, trains had to be taken on trains and only then to expresses. Obviously time-keeping was of prime importance but few drivers in steam days ever possessed a watch. Often the first one they ever owned was the one they received as a retirement present! Many drivers used the station clocks and even the clocks on church towers to check whether they were keeping to time. Others who knew their engines well could judge their speed almost precisely.

Although it wasn't possible to make tea on an engine, making a brew was the last thing to do before setting off. It long runs to places such as Scotland or the West Country and these trips were fraught with danger and angst. The drivers' wives would never know for sure when their husbands would be coming home from these lodging turns, as they were known. Food rationing could often make provision of meals for drivers and firemen away from home tricky, too, but eventually relief points were established at major stations where tins of sausages, sardines and soup were made available.

LOCOMOTIVE BUILDERS

■

IT WOULD BE HARD TO FIND a corner of Lancashire that did not feel the impact of the coming of the railway but perhaps those places that grew from virtually nothing to become major places of employment felt the change the most. And perhaps the most important of these were the towns where the locomotives were built.

In 1830, the great Vulcan Foundry Locomotive Works were founded by Charles Tayleur, a Liverpool engineer and owner of the Bank Quay foundry in Warrington. Tayleur had already sold a locomotive to the L&MR for over £1,000 and was effectively in competition with Stephenson who was managing a locomotive works in Newcastle-on-Tyne at this time. Stephenson, however, was finding it extremely difficult to transport heavy locomotives from Newcastle to Lancashire for use on the railway. He had already brought 60 'steady and sober' men down from the North-East to operate the locomotives and so bought into what became an arrangement of equals with Tayleur. A factory was to be built exactly halfway between Liverpool & Manchester in Newton-le-Willows. Stephenson became a partner in 1832 and in the same year, the first locomotives, *Tayleur* and *Stephenson*,

were delivered to the North Union Railway. These were followed in quick succession by three locomotives for the Warrington & Newton Railway: *Warrington*, *Vulcan* and *Newton*. Making a name for itself very quickly, the Vulcan foundry went on to supply the London & Greenwich Railway with its first locomotive and the *Jacob Perkins* for the Stanhope & Tyne Railway. In 1837, *Vulcan*, *Aelos* and *Pacchus* were delivered to the Great Western Railway, these being of broad (7 ft) gauge.

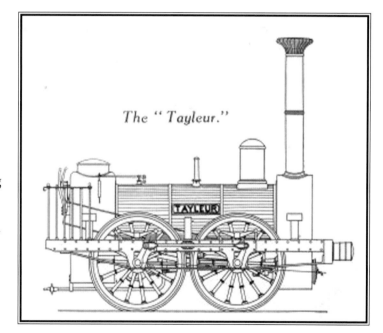

The "Tayleur."

■ *The 1830s' locomotive,* Tayleur. *(Ian Edwards Collection)* ■

■ *A 1950s' view of the Vulcan Works.* (Author's collection) ■

continued throughout the later years of the 19th century, with the workforce rising from 537 in 1865 to 1,390 by 1906.

During the 1914–1918 war, the foundry undertook a large amount of armament work and this was repeated again for a number of years prior to the Second World War when the works was engaged to produce tanks and other munitions for the War Department, along with torpedoes and gun mechanisms for the Admiralty. But, by the 1930s, the works were again concentrating on building locomotives for Britain, India, Argentina and China, (one for the latter is now preserved in the National Railway Museum, York). By this time, the workforce had risen to over 4,000.

In the Second World War, locomotive production remained a priority and no fewer than 390 'Austerity' 2-8-0 locomotives were constructed for the Ministry of Supply for the use of the War Department. The labour force in April 1944 reached an all-time high of 4,128 (including 850 women, twice the number number employed in the First World War). At the end of hostilities in 1945, locomotives were again manufactured, with the

Soon Vulcan's reputation was worldwide. The construction of eight 2-4-0 locomotives for the Great Indian Peninsular Railway in 1852 saw the beginning of a long association with the railways of India which, in the next hundred years, resulted in 2,750 locomotives being delivered to the sub-continent, (an average of one a fortnight). The first locomotive for the Japanese railways was built in 1872 and expansion

'Liberation' class locomotives built and delivered in 1946 for the rebuilding of continental Europe.

In 1955, the Vulcan Foundry merged with the English Electric Company Ltd. Following a large-scale reorganisation, the works made a significant contribution to the modernisation of British Railways, delivering over 900 diesel and electric locomotives between 1957 and 1968. English Electric became part of the GEC group of companies in 1968 and locomotive construction finally ceased in 1970. Later the factory was acquired by M.A.N. (B. & W. Diesel) Ltd. but was closed at the end of 2002. The buildings were demolished and the site cleared around 2007 but, whilst the sheds have gone, the village that housed its workers still remains.

Built at the same time as the works, Vulcan Village comprised six 'rows' of cottages named after major towns and cities, with the village originally having its own post office, school, laundry and public house, though only the last of these now remains. For a long time, every leap year, a toll was extracted from through traffic on 29th February. The village was sold during the 1970s to the Maritime Housing Association and has subsequently been extensively modernised. The houses are of a uniform cream colour and though slightly small for modern tastes, continue to command a quite striking and unusual appearance. Period notices, including a curious prohibition of singing, adorn the gable ends of the houses on Derby Row, whilst the last house on Manchester Row incorporates a magnificent representation, in stone, of *Vulcan*, which had been removed from the works.

Rather less well-known, but actually of an even earlier date

than the Vulcan Foundry, was the Haigh Foundry, just a couple of miles to the north of Wigan.

A forge at Brock Mill, by the River Douglas in Wigan, existed before 1766. By 1775 a foundry had been established half a mile downstream. In 1788, both were acquired by the Earl of Balcarres who formed a partnership to expand the two businesses and build blast furnaces at the Haigh Foundry site. Whilst the iron smelting was not to last, the foundry and forge slowly prospered and began to produce what were known locally as 'fire engines' – beam pumping engines for local collieries. In 1804, Robert Daglish was appointed chief engineer and his engineering skill and inventiveness soon made an impact.

In 1812, Daglish built Lancashire's first locomotive at Haigh. Modelled on Blenkinsop's *Yorkshire Horse*, it was to work trains from John Clarke's Orrell and Winstanley coal pits to the Leeds & Liverpool Canal. It worked very well, so much so that Daglish built two more before the end of 1816; one apparently able to operate purely by its steam. It was reported that two of these locomotives remained in use until the collieries closed in 1852. Haigh Foundry was acquiring a deserved reputation; it was becoming skilled at casting ever larger steam cylinders and the forge wrought the parts which couldn't be cast.

Exactly how many locomotives were built will probably never be known but the total was probably between 110 and 120. Many were for main-line railway companies such as the Grand Union, London & Birmingham, Birmingham & Gloucester and, closer to home, the Manchester & Bolton Railway. Intriguingly, despite the Vulcan Works just having been opened, Haigh also supplied three 2-2-0 locomotives to the Liverpool & Manchester Railway in 1836, these being named *Vesuvius*, *Lightning* and *Cyclops*.

Locomotives were only part of the business. Haigh Foundry was becoming a major player, supplying large, cast-iron, swing bridges and ironwork for Hull and Liverpool docks, and very large stationary steam engines for coal and metal mines. The foundry even dabbled in architectural ironwork as is hinted at by the huge hinges that still remain at the entrance to the site.

One problem Haigh had to overcome was that the works lay in the valley bottom and the only road out was very steep. In 1848, a massive beam engine (possibly the largest in the world at that date) had

■ *The bridge that carried railway traffic to the once great Haigh Foundry. (Author)* ■

reputedly needed 48 horses to drag its components up the hill. The answer was a railway, linking both foundry and forge to the nearby Haigh colliery railways. The line ran through what are now the grounds of Haigh Hall and followed the course of a former mill leat which at one time helped power the foundry. By 1869, however, the Lancashire Union Railway's Whelley Loop cut right across the foundry line and the LUR was obliged to provide another railway which connected with

the new route at Haigh Junction.

By now, Haigh Foundry was better known for building winding engines but had also expanded into brick and tile making. Contrary to popular belief, the foundry continued to make locomotives and even tendered for the Festiniog Railway's 'Prince' class. One structure it almost certainly didn't build, despite rumours to the contrary, was the great Laxey Wheel on the Isle of Man. It has even been suggested that the wheel is embossed with the words 'Made in Wigan'. However, an archivist with the Manx National Heritage has since stated that the wheel was constructed by the 'Vauxhall Foundry, Liverpool and the Mersey Iron Works, Ellesmere Port'.

By the late 1870s, the market was less buoyant and an economic depression in the early 1880s hit Haigh hard. Their lease was given up and the works closed in January 1885. The railway, however, continued in use until 1919, serving a coal yard and some tenants of the foundry buildings. Many of its employees are thought to have found new employment at the wagon works being developed at Ince, a couple of miles to the south.

Delightfully, most of the buildings survive at Haigh, along with two cast iron river bridges, one stone overbridge and almost the whole route of the 1869 railway. In one corner of the site, an iron foundry (J.T. & E. Castings) was still operating in 2010. Brock Mill forge, sadly, didn't survive and all traces were swept away by a rather inappropriate gated housing development in the 1990s.

****

By 1846 the Lancashire & Yorkshire Railway (LYR) had developed a locomotive and carriage/wagon works at Miles Platting, just east of Manchester. However, a fire at this site in 1873 meant that the carriage and wagon works were transferred to a new site at Newton Heath in 1877. A football club started by the railway workers in Newton Heath was the forerunner of the present-day Manchester United club. Meanwhile, the locomotive sheds at Miles Platting were

salvaged and the company continued to be responsible for the Lancashire & Yorkshire Railway's locomotives (along with the Locomotive Department at Victoria Station, Manchester). Although it was then able to concentrate on building locomotives, Miles Platting was still overwhelmed by demand and resorted to commissioning some privately-built locomotives. With little potential for expanding the facilities at Miles Platting's cramped site, a new location was sought to accommodate a modern works that could meet the demand and a site was identified at Horwich, just north of Bolton.

Horwich Works was built on 142 hectares of land bought in April 1884 for £36,000. An additional £4,600 also had to be paid for the diversion of the planned route of the Thirlmere aqueduct, which carried and indeed still does carry drinking water from the Lake District to Manchester. For rail access to the site, a branch line was constructed between September 1886 and 1st July 1887. It ran north-west of Blackrod station, through the works complex and on towards the north-east, under Chorley New Road to the site of the former Horwich terminus. Rivington House, the first of several workshops was well over 100 yards long and opened in February 1887. An 18-inch gauge railway, with an amazing 7½ miles of track, was built to carry materials around the works complex, modelled on a similar system at Crewe Works on the London and North Western Railway, with two tiny 0-4-0 tank locomotives bought from Beyer Peacock in 1887 to haul stores trains around the site. Six more were acquired at intervals up to 1901; the first being bought from Beyer Peacock, but the remainder were built at Horwich. From 1930 they were gradually withdrawn from service. The last, *Wren*, (a Beyer

■ *A narrow gauge locomotive stands in front of the loco works sheds at Horwich, now part of the designated conservation area. (Author's collection)* ■

Peacock engine) was withdrawn in 1961 and is preserved at the National Railway Museum in York.

The LYR sold 81 hectares of its original site to provide housing for its workers. In September 1885, a number of new streets were laid out and named after prominent engineers. The Railway Mechanics' Institute at Horwich opened on 15th December 1888. The new factory became the largest employer in Horwich, and retains much of its original elements today.

Construction of Horwich Works began in January 1888 and finished on 20th February 1889. The whole complex was in full operation by 1892 and the works became world famous for the quality of its craftsmanship. It became responsible not only for the LYR's locomotive building, but also for repair, mechanical, electrical and hydraulic engineering. Within its first ten years, it had produced 677 new locomotives. The first steam locomotive to be built at Horwich was a 2-4-2 tank engine (No. 1008).

In 1922 the close working relationship of the LYR and the London & North Western Railway (LNWR) was cemented by their amalgamation, with the LYR taking the LNWR title. One year later, in 1923, they collectively became part of the London, Midland and Scottish Railway (LMS). Although the effects on Horwich were not immediate, the existence of large-scale works at Crewe and Derby meant that the LMS would later look to centralise its operations to avoid duplication of work. By 1927 the telegraph shop, signal shops and points and crossing shop had all closed down at Horwich, with work transferred to other LMS sites.

Locomotive building continued at Horwich, though in 1931 it was temporarily suspended due to the economic downturn.

As the slump hit the locomotive building industry, Horwich focused on repairs. With the closure of the Newton Heath depot in 1932, it also took on the repairs of the local Electric Motor Units. Horwich was given over to ammunitions production, as well as production of vehicle and plane parts, during the Second World War and locomotive production did not resume until 1944. Following nationalisation Horwich became part of British Railways (London Midland Region).

While repair work continued, Horwich experienced not only a steady decline in the demand for maintenance of steam locomotives, but also an eventual cessation of general locomotive building. In 1952 work began on its first BR Standard locomotive but, by 1957, it was all over. Steam had been superseded and, by 1958, Horwich had built its first diesel shunters. This transition was short-lived, however, and by 1962 Horwich had also built its last diesel locomotive. Locomotive repair ceased at Horwich in May 1964, and the site was then used for train carriage repairs. The branch line to Horwich station closed on 30th January 1967. The erecting shop was cut in two in 1981 in order to construct a new traverser but despite this investment the works finally closed in 1983.

In recognition of its historical value, the site has been designated as the 'Horwich Locomotive Works Conservation Area' which will hopefully mean that it will never suffer the same fate as Vulcan. It also includes two significant buildings outside the original works – the dining room on Gooch Street (later the Lancashire & Yorkshire Arms) and the former cottage hospital on Brunel Street.

THE EARLY COMMUTERS

—— ■ ——

IT WAS CUSTOMARY AT ANY TIME up until the early 20th century to live as close as possible, generally less than an hour's walk, to your place of work. In the 21st century we travel further to work than we have ever done. Gradually, between these two periods of time, grew a phenomenon that few love and many resent, that of commuting. At first, train travel was too expensive for the average working man but fares gradually came down thanks to competition and William Gladstone's 1844 Railway Act, which obliged every company to supply at least one train daily at the cost of no more than 1d a mile, so eventually regular journeys from home to a place of work became possible.

Histories of commuting are few and far between. The word *commuter* itself derives from the early days of rail travel in US cities such as New York, Philadelphia, Boston and Chicago, where, in the 1840s, the railways started to charge regular travellers a reduced or 'commuted' fare into the city. Normally, the longer the period, the cheaper the cost per day, as still remains the case with our modern 'season' tickets. Whilst fewer children nowadays enjoy the pleasure of travelling to and from school by rail – and what fun those distant days were

– it is probably true to say that more people commute from Lancashire's villages and smaller towns to our cities than at any time in the past. Let us now take a look at the stories behind some of the better known 'commutes' in the county.

Perhaps few people in St Annes, Lancashire, were ever aware of their unique commuter service – 'the only club train in the world'. Every day a very special train used to run between Manchester and Blackpool; a train which consisted of a number of superbly-appointed carriages, reserved for the members of the Lytham, St Annes and Blackpool Travelling Club, and rightly named 'the club train'.

Around 1901, wealthy merchants and well-to-do businessmen from St Annes had found it extremely inconvenient travelling to and from their place of business, especially in the summer months, when all trains on the Blackpool line were naturally full. An attempt was made by the railway company to overcome the difficulty by reserving a number of compartments specifically for their use. However, this didn't satisfy people as it meant that they had to walk up and down the platform searching for one of the few reserved compartments. Consequently, some of the regular passengers banded together into a club and approached the company with the suggestion that it should place a number of saloon carriages at the disposal only of the members of the said club. The club, for its part, guaranteed a membership of forty individuals, who were prepared to pay a fee to the railway company that was by some margin in excess of the ordinary first-class season ticket.

After some negotiation, the company agreed to the terms and the club train sprang into being, providing special saloon cars dedicated to the use of these rather privileged passengers. The saloons were serviced by an attendant who would ensure that a member's favourite armchair was kept free for that individual's use. Members enjoyed the benefits of newspapers and a range of refreshments en route to and from Manchester. On both outward and return journeys the average speed (including station stops) was over 40 mph, a very high figure for this type of service. During the inter-war years two massive, smooth riding, twelve-wheeled bogie saloons as used on the London–Liverpool Atlantic Boat Trains were provided for the Blackpool Club service. Like all other clubs, it produced its own rules, one of which clearly outlined the sought-after exclusivity: 'No member is allowed to bring a guest or friend on the train, even if he is prepared to pay treble the 1st class fare.' Perhaps even more unusual was a rule prohibiting travellers from opening the windows; instead anyone needing fresh air had to instruct an attendant to open some ventilators.

It can be seen that provision of good train services by the LNWR between the Fylde and Manchester encouraged affluent Manchester businessmen to establish their homes on the coast and commute daily to their work in the city. In this way the Manchester men could emulate the lifestyle of many of their London counterparts. The 'Blackpool to Manchester Club Train' was both the fastest service on the line and one which, in the manner described above, effectively excluded all undesirable travelling companions. This novel service stood the test of time and the First World War but not the Second World War.

It is not unfair to suggest that our next commuter railway

attracted a slightly less elite clientele. By the 1880s, Liverpool's dock network was virtually complete. So, too, was the congestion along the dock road, as carriages, omnibuses, lorries, carts and drays all plied the same narrow roads. Numerous railway crossings which connected goods stations and dockside lines only added to the confusion. Amongst the many problems encountered was the choice of motive power. Steam was considered too dangerous to the many flammable cargoes within range of locomotive sparks. So, as early as 1893, an electric commuter railway was operating – the Liverpool Overhead Railway – always known locally as 'Paddy's Umbrella'. Extensive bomb damage was inflicted during the Blitz but it was quickly repaired to maintain the smooth running of the docks. In 1955, however, the curved deck plates which supported the track were reported as being in need of replacement at an approximate cost of £2 million. This was beyond the financial resources of the company, who looked to the City Council and the Mersey Docks and Harbour Board for assistance. No adequate solution could be found and, despite rigorous public protests, the railway closed on 30th December 1956. Rescue attempts continued until September 1957, when the dismantlers moved in. Virtually nothing remains now except part of the site at Dingle station, the line's eastern terminus.

The Liverpool Overhead Railway hit the headlines again in July 2012 when part of a tunnel at the Dingle end collapsed, leading to the evacuation of over 100 homes in the local area. The collapse involved an area of the tunnel roof measuring around 20 metres wide by 10 metres.

By the mid 19th century, the Lancashire & Yorkshire

■ *A 1930s' view of the Underground Island Platform at Dingle on the Liverpool Overhead Railway.* ■

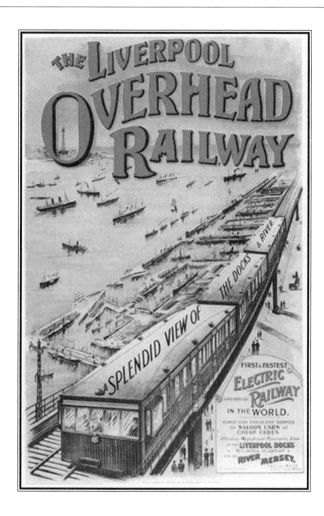

■ *An early 20th-century poster for the Liverpool Overhead Railway. (Author's collection)* ■

Railway was starting to complete what amounted to quite a dense network of suburban lines in and around Manchester. North of the city was a steeply-graded branch from Middleton Junction to Oldham Werneth which was opened in 1942 and which was extended to Oldham Mumps in 1847. In 1863 a line from the east end of Rochdale via Shaw to Oldham was opened. The Cheetham Hill loop line from Victoria to Thorpes Bridge Junction was built in 1877, avoiding steep gradients on the Miles Platting line and in 1904 the LYR opened a new short line to bring trains from the Bury line into the terminal platforms on the south side of Victoria station.

The spread of street tramways on radial routes from central Manchester and their electrification in the early 1900s, however, combined with frequent services and low fares compared to the trains, caused a marked loss of railway passengers on the suburban services. To counteract this, the LYR electrified the Bury via Prestwich line in 1916. This originally extended a further 3¾ miles further north to Holcombe Brook, where the LYR had experimented with an overhead electrification scheme. The scheme was paid for by Dick, Kerr & Company of Preston as they needed to demonstrate their electric traction supply and motive power equipment in the hope of winning a huge order from Brazil. The route was electrified with overhead wires energised at 3,500vDC and two trains were built to operate the passenger service at the LYR works at Newton Heath. A 15-minute interval service between Bury and Holcombe Brook could be maintained by the use of only one set. However, this was dismantled after a few years in favour of the third rail system.

■ *A viaduct on the Holcombe Brook branch line. Although the branch always remained single track, the viaduct's stone pillars were built wide enough to accommodate a second line that was never needed.* (Author) ■

Of course the railways were also used to get to places of recreation. George Bradshaw, an engraver and printer at Manchester, was the first to realise that what people might like, therefore, was a handy guide covering the whole railway network rather than just one individual company's route. So, on 19th October 1839, the first of Bradshaw's popular monthly *Railway Time Tables and Assistant to Railway Travelling* was published.

By the 1860s travellers from Lancashire could reach the Lakes, the Peak District or the hills of North Yorkshire, but what was unofficially known as the 'hikers' railway' was a little closer to home. The West Pennine Moors around Chorley have always been popular with those striving for a spot of fresh air and a good brisk ramble in fine surroundings with extensive views. On a typical summer's weekend, dozens of ramblers still head for White Coppice or Rivington in cars, whilst others might take a bus. Yet there used to be a railway line that would take you and drop you off almost on the doorstep. It closed to passengers in January 1960 but in its heyday, up to a dozen steam trains per day would trundle up and down a 1 in 60 gradient between the two towns of Chorley and Blackburn. There were also three local services each way on Sundays.

The line was commissioned by the Lancashire Union Railway (LUR) and the LYR who were keen to link the mills of East Lancashire with the coal mines of Wigan without having to go all the way round via Preston. Work started in 1860 but it was not until 1869 that the line officially opened. It cost over £500,000 – a fortune in the Victorian era. This line also had a nine-arch viaduct carried trains 40 ft above the Leeds–Liverpool Canal close to the mill at Botany Bay which was removed to make way for the M61 motorway and whose demolition in 1968 attracted thousands of onlookers. A three-arch viaduct over the A674 between Feniscowles and Cherry Tree on the outskirts of Blackburn still cuts an impressive sight at the opposite end of the line.

■ *The Douglas viaduct on the Whelley Loop line; Wigan's former north/south avoiding line.* ■

ROSSENDALE & THE MANCHESTER SHIP CANAL

∎

As a county with such a large industrial base, it is not difficult to find evidence of the railways that served it. Coal mining was a huge business and obviously closely linked to the railways: the railways needed coal to operate and the mines needed the railways to get the coal to where it was needed. It could well be argued that when dieselisation started to break that link, it was the start of the decline for both industries.

This chapter, though, will concentrate on two of Lancashire's slightly lesser-known industries, both with remarkably extensive railway systems. Later we will examine the Manchester Ship Canal and its railway system but first let us head to the hills above Rossendale. Now largely a place of peace and solitude, this was once the site of busy and noisy quarrying, and one quarry is still active here on the east side.

Stone has been quarried in Rossendale since at least the 14th century and probably long before that. There are records of stone being sold in Rossendale in 1341 and of rents being paid for quarries in the middle of the 15th century. This would

have obviously been small-scale, and sourced on an ad hoc basis whenever a building project required materials. Farmers who wanted stone for a building or the countless dry stone walls that criss-cross the landscape would find an outcrop of stone as near as possible and take stone from there by horse-drawn cart or on a sled.

The stone splits easily into thin sheets suitable for roofing slates and these slates were a valuable commodity. The difference between the grey slate roofs of the older houses in Rossendale and the reddish roof tiles of more modern construction can still be seen when looking down from the tops of the moors. These slates, placed on end, were also used as boundary fences.

As the growing towns of the Industrial Revolution demanded more and more stone, bigger quarries were developed and quarrymen were soon arriving from all parts of the country. On the 1881 census, people from places such as Norfolk and Cornwall, with their own long-standing tradition of mining and quarrying, (one gravestone in Bacup cemetery is a memorial to a Cornish quarryman) came to Lancashire for employment. The most remarkable statistic, though, is that over 20,000 workers and their families from Ireland settled in the area. Every day hundreds of quarrymen would set off to work from the valley bottom and climb the steep inclines, wearing jackets, waistcoats and trousers made of heavy moleskin or corduroy to keep out the wind and rain.

With the coming of the railway to Rossendale in 1846, and to Bacup by 1851, quarries rapidly expanded in the area and, for some years, entire hillsides were carved away to supply stone for towns and cities all over Britain and abroad. Perhaps

■ *The incline at Cloughfold, near Rawtenstall, part of the Rossendale tramways.* (Bertram Baxter collection) ■

the most distinctive feature of Rossendale quarries was the extensive network of narrow gauge moorland tramways. There was no 'network' across the moor, just a series of lines, with formations marked out in places by slate fences; some standard gauge tracks and others of around 3 ft running from the quarries down to where their stone could be offloaded. There was one line built 'around the contours' from a point above the west portal of Bacup Tunnel to a point above Britannia, but its purpose has never really been clear. These tracks were, in effect, a system linking distant moorland tramways directly to the main railway lines in the valley bottom. Many were of quite some length – the longest individual system was over 11 miles long and reached a height of over 1,500 ft on the moor tops.

Accurate records of opening and closure dates were not carefully kept. Most of the tramroads and inclines linking the quarries to the Bury–Bacup line, however, would have been up and running by the 1870s, if not before, as datable evidence exists of locomotives being bought and sold by the quarry owners. Connections via inclines at Britannia and Facit would have followed soon after the opening of what was known as the 'New Line' to Bacup in 1881.

The Rossendale stone industry mushroomed and the main entrepreneurs were the large companies of Henry Heys, Brooks & Brooks, and Siddalls. Mr Heys, an entrepreneur and architect of stone buildings, was a remarkable character. Although he could neither read nor write (he signed his name with a mark), Heys had the remarkable ability to calculate and estimate the yardages of stone required to complete particular buildings. At India Mill, Bacup, he correctly assessed and measured up the stone requirements in a couple of hours. An astonished surveyor, hired by the mill owner, said it would have taken him three weeks to do that sort of measurement.

Little is known of the locomotives and the crews that operated these lines, though it is known that they were transferred from one route to another quite frequently, dependent on demand. More is known about the Scout Moor Tramway, which ran from a quarry (and also a reservoir) on the south-west side of the moors to a landsale yard just above Edenfield. This was a 3 ft gauge line, owned by James Whittaker & Son, which opened in 1880 and ran profitably enough until an extensive landslip occurred in the late 1930s, taking several yards of rail some distance down the hillside. Perhaps due to the coming war, the landslip was never made good (lengthy pieces of rail may still be seen on the landslip) but closure was clearly not intended as a new cylinder had just been delivered for one of the tiny Bagnall four-coupled saddle tanks that operated the line. The Bagnall sat in its shed, slumbering undisturbed alongside the new cylinder, for over 20 years until 1961 when it was dragged out and cut up for scrap. Even more remarkable was the survival of *Excelsior*. This was a 2-2-0 well tank, looking more like a traction engine, which is unsurprising as it was built by Aveling & Porter, famous and long-standing constructors and suppliers of such vehicles. *Excelsior* was believed to have not been in steam since 1914, but still sat in its siding patiently awaiting developments. Its historical value having been recognised, *Excelsior* was saved from the cutters' torch and moved to the Aveling headquarters. It can now be seen on view at the

Hollycombe Working Steam Museum at Liphook in Hampshire.

The Rossendale quarry industry became uneconomic around the time of the First World War, and gradually all the tracks were lifted. However, the spectacular moorland tramways have probably attracted more attention than the quarries themselves. They appeal not only to local historians and railway enthusiasts, but also the general walker – the track-beds often remain as rights of way and make for superb upland walking. Many of the 'Valley of Stone' heritage walks make use of them as the best link routes between the quarries. The abandoned tramways have a fascination all of their own, with miles of sharp twists and turns following the contours. Although their earthworks are relatively light, they remain remarkable feats of engineering.

Let us now move on to a very different enterprise. As discussed earlier, the two great cities of Manchester and Liverpool have long held a fierce rivalry, seen more often these days on the football pitch. Throughout the 19th century, the Manchester Corporation and local businessmen had been jealous of Liverpool's status as a major port and longed to find some way for sea-going ships to reach their city as well. The new railways, though excellent for passengers and 'native' commodities, required expensive dock and exchange facilities for goods coming by ship. This adversely affected the profits to be made by Mancunian entrepreneurs. As early as 1838, plans for a larger canal were being proposed by Sir John Rennie but it wasn't until 1877 that Daniel Adamson gained the support and finance to build what we know as the Manchester Ship Canal. On 1st January 1894, after many years of delays, a flotilla of boats left the canal's western entrance at Eastham, bound for Manchester. An official opening by Queen Victoria followed on 21st May of that year.

Now, if you were asked to name the owner of the largest private railway company in Britain after 1948, the Manchester Ship Canal might not be the first name that came to mind. But, surprisingly, it was.

The Manchester Ship Canal Railway (MSCR) was built to service freight to and from the canal's docks and nearby industrial estates, and connect to the various railway companies that had track near the canal. What needs to be remembered is that the canal did not merely serve Manchester but a number of other ports along the way, as well as one other major town, Warrington. In hindsight, however, industry was slow to settle on the banks of the MSCR, with only a few major industries taking advantage of the facilities before 1945. A chemical plant was built on Wigg Island, east of Runcorn, and an aluminium factory constructed in Latchford, as part of the war effort. The railway was generally at its busiest in wartime, and tonnages carried then often exceeded those carried on the canal itself. The railway remained very busy throughout the 1940s; indeed, during 1949 it was still carrying 7½ million tons of traffic, but ten years later this figure had dropped to just 4 million, declining further every succeeding year.

The MSCR did not form one continuous route. Running from Manchester Docks, it went west past Barton and Irlam to Latchford, where a connecting line reached the L&NWR routes in Warrington. There was then a short gap before a line from Acton Bridge Junction followed the canal north of

A Stanier seen here at Trafford Park in the late 1960s. (Glenn Morris)

Moore to reach a point just short of the old quay in Runcorn. The westernmost section from Ellesmere Port to Eastham did not open until 1967, some years after most of the rest of the system had closed.

Unlike most other railway companies in the UK, it was not nationalised in 1948. The MSCR, like the Mersey Docks and Harbour Board and the Port of London Authority, to name but two, were privately-owned industrial systems and thus not subject to the Transport Act of that year. At its peak it had 790 employees, 75 locomotives, 2,700 wagons and more than 200 miles of track. The MSCR was able to receive and despatch goods trains to and from all the UK's main line railway systems, using connecting junctions at three points in the terminal docks. Two were to the north of the canal, operated by the Lancashire & Yorkshire Railway and the London & North Western Railway and one was to the south, operated by the Cheshire Lines Committee.

Let us also spend a little time considering Trafford Park. As the name suggests, it was once truly a park, consisting of 1,200 acres of farmland and meadowland surrounding Trafford Hall, an environment frequented by deer and other smaller wildlife. Its transformation into what was to become the first purpose-built industrial estate in the country was masterminded by one Mr Marshall Stevens. Surrounded on one side by the Bridgewater Canal, after the construction of the Ship Canal the park became rather isolated, almost an island, and was sold to a financier named Hooley who, with Marshall, was quick to begin developments. A railway connection between the park and the docks was put in place by 1898 and, as various factories were constructed, was continuously being added to and extended.

The Co-operative Wholesale Society (CWS) had a major food packing factory and a flour mill there; it also had soap and candle works further up the canal at Lower Irlam. The Ford Motor Company produced the Model T Ford there and the British Westinghouse Electric Company (which later became Metropolitan Vickers) made turbines and generators. Trafford Park expanded rapidly during the First World War and was used extensively by the Ministry of Munitions. However, by the end of 1914, one third of the workforce had volunteered to join up. This resulted in a serious loss of skills in Trafford Park and the War Office began to refuse to enlist factory workers. Employment in Trafford Park also fell significantly during the economic depression of the 1920s and 1930s.

Eventually, though, more new factories and distribution hubs opened. These included W. & R. Jacob & Co. Ltd., biscuit (and cream cracker) manufacturers, and the Lancashire Dynamo and Motor Company. Many of the factories in Trafford Park were quickly turned to war use. For example, the Metrovick factory was rapidly adapted to make munitions. During the Second World War, employment in Trafford Park rose from 50,000 to 75,000. After the war, Brooke Bond moved its tea packaging factory to the canalside in Ordsall, Kellogg's started making cornflakes, whilst ICI built its first purpose-built factory for the mass production of penicillin. Employment also held up well in the 1940s and 1950s, but the 1960s brought the first closures.

Returning to the railway, a number of difficulties were encountered because of the size and diversity of the different premises. Some could be built in neat rectangular rows but because they all required rail access, some had to be built at what now seem rather odd angles. The laying out of the roads was straightforward but with the railways it was more complex. A minimum curve radius of 200 ft was agreed upon but this still required a special breed of engine. The MSC's steam locomotives were designed to negotiate the tight-radius curves of the tracks on which they ran; the middle wheels of the 0-6-0 arrangement were flangeless, and the coupling rods had a hinged central section that permitted several inches of lateral play. A fleet of diesel locomotives was purchased between 1959 and 1966, but were soon surplus to requirements and a number were moved to Ellesmere Port and Stanlow.

■ *A former siding next to offices at Trafford Park.* (Author) ■

EXCURSIONS AND HOLIDAY TRAFFIC

WHILST THESE DAYS REGULAR scheduled passenger services are busier than at any time in the last 70 years, fewer and fewer excursion trains now operate. Part of the reason is logistical, with fixed units and limited paths available on the main routes, there simply is not the capacity. However, in Lancashire, the Hellifield route north of Blackburn and the Carnforth to Wennington route remain popular destinations for 'main line steam' and details of such services can easily be found in the railway press or via an internet search.

So let us spend some time tracing the history of the excursion train. Once again we will start by taking a look at the L&MR. Perhaps because there was an expectation that a railway (like a canal or a turnpike road, but not a railway in latter days) would be a common carrier open to all, a range of different groups was keen to take advantage of the new facility.

By the summer of 1831, the Liverpool & Manchester Railway was carrying tens of thousands of Sunday school children on excursions, plus there were special trips between the two cities at Whitsuntide and other holidays. Once the Bolton & Leigh Railway was up and running ten years later in

1941, a return excursion ticket from Bolton to Liverpool cost a surprisingly large 2s 6d (12½p). Special trains also operated to Newton races. Contemporary reports describe Newton race day as more of a fair, with boxing booths, sideshows and other attractions, alongside the racing itself. The course was actually in what became Earlestown, not far from Market Street and thus was convenient for the station of that name. Newton was recognised as one of the best racecourses of its time but it was not enclosed and therefore could never support itself by charging an entry fee. Eventually the racing was moved a couple of miles north to Haydock Park, which opened in February 1899. From the start the new course had its own station on the Great Central Railway's St Helens branch, right next to the course entrance.

Lancashire's most famous horse race is, of course, the Grand National which first took place in 1837. There was no nearby rail service here though until 1849, when the first Aintree station (later renamed Fazackerley and still in use) opened on what was to become the Lancashire & Yorkshire Railway's Liverpool to Preston via Wigan route. Twenty years later another station opened on the Cheshire Lines Committee's route to Hunt's Cross but both these were some distance from the course entrance. A better sited station was opened on a freight-only line close to the LYR route. This was perhaps one of the most peculiar set-ups of any station – there were no proper platforms but the eastbound track was raised to 'platform height' and filled in with gravel between the tracks and used for passengers who arrived and departed on trains using the westbound tracks – just about adequate for the one day in the year it was used for this purpose. The latter station, known simply as Aintree racecourse, was last used in 1962. At its peak the numbers of spectators carried were extraordinary: 91 trains, one arriving every two minutes at one or other station, disgorged their passengers in 1912 when *Jerry M* was victorious in the Grand National. It is more than likely that numbers were even higher in 1903 when King Edward VII was present to watch his horse, *Ambush II*, take part in the race.

Football has, since the 1880s, been the most well supported sport in the county, with Lancashire teams dominant from the start of the Football League and right up to the present day, for much of the time. Railway companies were quick to pick up on the potential for business from away supporters wanting to follow their team and for trips to special occasion matches such as internationals and cup finals. One example was the FA Cup Final of 1904 between Manchester City and Bolton Wanderers held at Crystal Palace in London. Several companies ran services but the best remembered is the Great Central Railway whose advertising poster tempted you to 'watch Billy Murdoch secure the Cup for City' which, amazingly enough, he did. Wembley Stadium opened in 1923 when Bolton Wanderers were again involved (and again on the losing side). This game attracted about 200,000 people, twice the ground's capacity, with around 30 trains heading south for the day. The 1953 final (again with Bolton Wanderers on the losing side but this time beaten in an all-Lancashire affair by Blackpool) was one of the last 'all rail' excursions with 21 special trains from each town pressed into service.

Rugby League, particularly major Challenge Cup matches, could also generate significant traffic. The Challenge Cup final was first played at Wembley in 1929, when Wigan beat Dewsbury in front of a crowd of over 40,000 spectators. It is safe to assume that the great majority would have travelled by rail, but no records appear to exist of numbers of special trains. As late as 1961 twelve trains took St Helens supporters to Odsal stadium in Bradford for a Challenge Cup semi-final against Hull and a total of 34 additional services went to Wembley for the final when Saints were again victorious, this time against local rivals Wigan.

The mention of Sunday school excursions takes us on to discussing an early controversy. With Sunday being the only day off for most working people in the early to mid 19th century, that was the day railway companies felt they could run excursions profitably. However, despite them being sometimes popular with Sunday schools, such 'pleasure trips' became the subject of fierce criticism by Sabbatarians. Part of their argument revolved around the railway employees being made to work on what should have been their 'day of rest', but more so was the perceived need to keep the Sabbath as a day for sobriety, prayer and peaceful reflection – not quite the constituents of a typical day out in Blackpool! Such arguments continued right into the 20th century. As a result, some railway companies did go to great lengths to ensure that such day trips allowed time for 'attendance at a place of worship'.

A number of philanthropic and enlightened employers took the opportunity to treat their workers to a 'day trip' on special occasions. One such was Richard Cobden, printer and politician credited for his efforts to achieve repeal of the Corn Laws in spite of opposition from then prime minister (and fellow Lancastrian) Sir Robert Peel. On finally celebrating the

■ *Heading for the coast in the 1950s – a Southport-bound excursion passes Gathurst.* (Author's collection) ■

repeal, in 1848, Cobden treated all his employees in Chorley to a day trip to Fleetwood (together with a day's pay) on the newly-opened Preston & Wyre Railway. In the same year, a Blackburn newspaper reported that Messrs Hopwood, cotton mill owners, had taken no fewer than 1,200 employees on a day trip to Blackpool, with bread and cheese provided as sustenance for the journey. The following year Smethurst's, textile mill owners, again of Chorley, sent 800 people to Blackpool for the day accompanied by refreshments and with a band to lead them off the train.

So it is clear that by the 1840s, the seaside excursion was already proving popular. As early as 1842, a 27-coach train had run from Preston to the newly-opened station at Fleetwood, a short distance from the golden sands just down the coast at Blackpool. This train carried over 2,000 Sunday school pupils and their teachers who apparently were 'engaged in singing hymns throughout the journey'. Indeed by 1844 the *Preston Chronicle* was reporting that 'Cheap Trains and Pleasure Excursions are now all the go and fashion'. In 1849 the above Fleetwood train was dwarfed by one of no less than 55 carriages running from Rochdale via Bury, then along the newly-opened branch line to Blackpool itself. Though not meeting with the approval of the Duke of Wellington who deplored the new-found mobility of the 'great unwashed', others were more positive. One 19th-century commentator wrote that 'crowds of

An 1851 Lancashire & Yorkshire Railway notice offering excursions. (Ian Edwards collection) ■

poor people from the manufacturing towns find there is physic in the sea, combining all the virtues of the drugs in the doctor's shop and a cure for all varieties of disease'. But the sheer amount of travellers on these pioneering 1840s' excursions was testament to their early popularity.

These numbers of people and the carriages that brought them clearly needed a considerable degree of space and organisation. For example, on August Bank Holiday 1910, the terminus stations in Blackpool handled no fewer than 207 incoming and 216 outgoing trains between them, carrying an astonishing 195,000 passengers. Even this huge total was beaten on the corresponding day in 1938 when 451 special trains ran. Despite there being fifteen platforms at Blackpool North and a further fourteen at Blackpool Central (together with 34 parallel carriage sidings), delays were common. To minimise reversals and other unnecessary traffic movements, a through route between the stations was suggested, allowing a 'loop' system to be put into operation, but the Great War intervened before anything happened on the ground. It is also of interest that there was never a north to west curve off the Preston to Lancaster (West Coast Main Line) route. This led to the

■ *Morecambe's old station which was replaced by a more basic structure half a mile closer to Lancaster. The station is now used as an arts centre.* (Author) ■

unusual situation of trains from points north running through Preston twice, first southbound through the old East Lancs Railway platforms (now demolished), then after traversing a

A 1950s' holiday excursion reversing out of Blackpool Central station. (Glenn Morris)

loop via Lostock Hall and Farington Curve Junctions, northbound to access the Blackpool line, a cause of obvious confusion to the unwary passenger.

Other events of note that drew large excursion traffic included the Southport Flower Show which started in 1924 and was the largest in the world by 1939. Preston Guild, (a festival held every twenty years since 1542 apart from a ten-year delay between 1942 and 1952) still attracts huge numbers of visitors. In 1862 an estimated 500,000 day-trippers attempted to pass through what was still a rather small and undeveloped station, leading to overcrowding and considerable disquiet. For the 1882 festival, the adjacent goods station was brought into use as additional passenger accommodation which enabled things to run more smoothly and, by 1902, the station itself had been considerably enlarged and was better able to cope. In 1922 the station somehow managed to accommodate almost 500 special trains across the week, with over 550,000 return tickets to Preston being issued over the seven days.

One unusual event was the total eclipse of the sun on Sunday, 29th June 1927. It appears that North Yorkshire was the best viewpoint and, accordingly, the LNWR ran excursions from a range of Lancashire destinations. Unfortunately, none of the passengers saw anything of the eclipse. It was recorded that 'it was a crying shame that on such a notable day that nature would greet the thousands of travellers with such a frown. Rain came down in torrents for hours – some people never left their coaches; others commandeered every corner of the storm drenched station (Richmond) in their search for shelter.'

■ *A 1950s' timetable for Ribble Valley Line excursions from Blackburn.* ■

Early excursions were also run for what seems, from a modern viewpoint, much less pleasant events. A public hanging in Liverpool of a certain John Wilson, guilty of murder, in 1849 led the London & North Western Railway to arrange a number of additional services – all of which were 'densely packed'. A crowd of around 50,000 apparently displayed their 'usual levity' but were praised for keeping good order. Later that day, the murderer's clothes were removed and taken by train to Madame Tussaud's in London where they were to be placed on a wax model of the unfortunate Mr Wilson. Perhaps only slightly more palatable was bare knuckle boxing. Although it had already supposedly been banned, the London & North Western Railway ran trains from both Liverpool and Manchester to Wolverton where a fight was taking place between two deadly rivals, Caunt and Bendigo. Unlike the eclipse viewers, these excursionists certainly got their money's worth, the fight lasting an extraordinary 93 rounds before Bendigo was awarded the contest.

Not every special service produced the desired 'good day out'. One unfortunate accident involved three excursion trains carrying some 3,000 people on a day trip from East Lancashire to Salford and Belle Vue Gardens. Eleven people died and a hundred more injured in a collision close to Helmshore station, north of Ramsbottom. On the return trip, the first train ran through smoothly but the second train with about 1,000 passengers and 31 carriages got to Helmshore where it stopped to let out some passengers. When the guard released the brakes, there was a jerk and the sixteen rearmost carriages broke away from the train and started sliding back down the line on a gradient towards Ramsbottom. Mr Shaw, the station superintendent, saw what had happened and unhooked the engine from the train in order to go down the other line to warn the third train but, unfortunately, he was too late. The carriages had already run 400 yards down the line and collided with the oncoming third train.

The beginning of the end of high volume holiday traffic was perhaps marked by the end of petrol rationing in 1950. Whilst numbers remained huge by modern standards, a decline had set in as car ownership gradually increased, closely followed by the development of cheap package holidays to Spain and other places where good weather could be guaranteed. By 1964 all Blackpool's traffic could be handled at North station, with Central being closed to allow construction of a huge car and coach park. Morecambe's excursion station at Euston Road had closed two years earlier.

Let me end this section with a strange story about Oldham dating from 1848. A day excursion to Blackpool was advertised, with tickets for some reason charged at 1s (5p) for ladies but 1s 6d (7½p) for gentlemen. The stationmaster at Oldham Mumps station soon noticed that some of the 'ladies' were not quite what they seemed; the offer of cheaper fares for the women had been enough to persuade certain of the men to dress in a rather unconventional manner! When inspectors were called in to investigate, they were apparently stampeded by a crowd of impatient passengers and were left on the ground covered in dust as the train departed.

THE HOTEL PIONEERS

I T IS NOT UNFAIR TO SAY that the railways pioneered the hotel industry in Britain (as opposed to the guest house or roadside inn). From the 1830s to the 1980s when the last 'British Transport Hotel' was sold off, the association between rail travel and luxury accommodation was clear. As late as 1970, British Transport was the fourth biggest provider of hotel rooms in Britain, just behind such noted names of the era as Strand Hotels and Trust House Forte.

In Lancashire there were city centre hotels in Manchester (the Midland) and Liverpool (the North Western, the Exchange Station Hotel and the Adelphi), whilst the L&NWR also at one time operated hotels in Lancaster and Preston, the latter jointly with the Midland Railway. These were sold off in 1929 and 1949 respectively. The Towneley Arms Hotel, adjacent to the former terminus at Longridge, was also railway-owned, as well as a number of non-residential inns generally next to stations. However, it is the two great seaside railway hotels of the county, in Fleetwood and Morecambe, that we shall look at a little more closely.

Fleetwood's crown jewel was, and perhaps still remains, the North Euston hotel. Built in 1841 and designed by Decimus Burton (named Decimus as he was a tenth son), it is a fine, semi-circular building in the most prime of locations overlooking Morecambe Bay and the Wyre Estuary. It was believed at the time that it would never be possible to link

■ *The Midland Hotel, Manchester, opened in 1903 to serve Manchester Central railway station.* (Author) ■

■ *The North Euston Hotel, Fleetwood, now a Grade II listed building. (Author)* ■

■ *The Towneley Arms, Longridge, was once part of Longridge railway station. (Author's collection)* ■

England and Scotland by rail, so the idea was that passengers would travel by train to the furthest possible point, to a new port at a new town – Fleetwood – named after Sir William Fleetwood Hesketh. After an overnight stay, passengers would then board a steamer bound for Ardrossan in Scotland. The construction of the railway over Shap Fell in the Lake District in 1847 soon ended this sea/rail link, however.

In 1859 the North Euston Hotel was bought by the War Department and became the School of Musketry for officers. The school closed down in 1867 and the building became officers' quarters for a garrison of troops located near the cemetery. By 1891, though, the fortunes of Fleetwood as a holiday destination had improved sufficiently for it to be reopened as a hotel. Although undoubtedly one of Fleetwood's most spectacular buildings, and indeed a reason in itself to visit the town, it can also be argued that it is partly glorious folly and part historical curiosity, but mostly a reminder that those visionary Victorians did not get everything right.

The North Euston was the first hotel anywhere to use a curved façade, which certainly adds to the dignity and ambience of the front-facing rooms within, though making the furnishing rather more awkward, and such a façade was later to be copied just up the coastline at Morecambe.

■ *The Midland Hotel, Morecambe, now designated a Transport Heritage Site.* (Author) ■

When the present Midland Hotel opened in Morecambe in 1933, it took the place of an earlier hotel, also called the Midland, which had occupied the site since 1848. By the 1840s, Morecambe was beginning to evolve from the old fishing village of Poulton-le-Sands into an embryonic holiday resort. The fishermen's cottages and small boarding houses were becoming insufficient to cope with the influx of visitors and there arose a need for purpose-built hotels.

In 1846 the 'Little' North Western Railway purchased land to the west of Poulton for the development of a port. The company also obtained permission to build a hotel as part of its scheme to construct a railway linking the new port with Yorkshire. The hotel was designed by Edward Paley, a local architect, and cost the grand and perhaps surprisingly high sum of £4,795, including furnishings. It was a two-storey building of grey stone, with green shuttered windows and contained 40 bedrooms. For a Victorian building, it had a distinctly Georgian look. Known initially as the North Western Hotel (its name was changed in 1871 when the Midland Railway took over the 'Little' North Western Railway), it stood in its own spacious grounds and catered for a clientele referred to as the 'carriage trade'. Although the more wealthy families might arrive by train, they would invariably be met at the station by their own horse-drawn vehicles laden with luggage and would then drive the short distance to the hotel entrance.

How peaceful a stay the guests enjoyed is a matter for conjecture. The main railway line to the harbour passed right next to the hotel and for the last 30 years of its existence they had to put up with the noise generated by the neighbouring

■ *The Midland Railway gatepost outside the Midland Hotel.* (Author) ■

ship-breakers yard of T.W. Ward. During the latter part of the 19th century and into the third decade of the 20th, Morecambe grew and prospered as a holiday resort, its development interrupted only by the First World War. As the 1920s drew to a close, it was apparent that the old Midland Hotel had become inadequate for the changing times.

The London, Midland and Scottish Railway Company was now responsible for the Midland Hotel and decided to replace the existing Victorian building with a more modern structure. In January 1932, it approved plans for a new hotel to be built on the seafront at a cost of just under £72,000. Bravely, the LMS saw Morecambe as an opportunity to make a radical new departure from traditional hotel design and selected the architect Oliver Hill to provide the company with 'a building of international quality in the modern style'. Work commenced in August 1932, the new building rising from the lawn in front of the old hotel before the latter was eventually demolished some months later. Hill's design was for a three-storey, curved structure which followed the line of the new municipal promenade, with its convex side towards the sea allowing good views from every room The concave side faced the railway station and was divided by a tower containing the hotel entrance and spiral staircase. The north end was finished off on the ground floor by what was, and again is today, a semi-circular café.

A contemporary observer described it as 'in complete harmony with its natural surroundings … it rises from the sea like a great white ship, gracefully curved'. Inside, the impression was one of space – from the open spiral staircase above with its cantilevered steps to the sparsely furnished entrance lounge ahead and, leading off it to the right, the sweeping curve of the dining room. Upstairs, the bedrooms were the latest word in luxury, while the flat roof was conceived as a solarium where guests could enjoy sunbathing in total seclusion.

At the outbreak of the Second World War, Morecambe became an important RAF station and the Midland was requisitioned by the Government for use as a military hospital. Valuable items were put into store and the interior of the building converted. On the ground floor the dining room became a large ward with some 40 beds, while the circular café was adapted to serve as a physiotherapy centre. Other rooms were used for operating theatres and recovery wards whilst additional beds were provided in Nissen huts erected in the hotel grounds.

After the war, the Midland was handed back to the LMS and re-opened to the public in July 1948. The hotel continued to operate for the next three years but was never particularly profitable. Following nationalisation of the railways, the British Transport Commission no longer saw the need for seaside hotels and asked Morecambe Corporation if it would be interested in buying the Midland but the offer was declined. It was eventually sold on in 1952 and on 25th July of that year, just nineteen years after it had first opened, the Midland Hotel passed out of railway hands. After several further changes of ownership, it was eventually purchased by a Manchester-based development company, Urban Splash, who proudly reopened the hotel on 1st June 2008.

THE WARTIME YEARS

——— ■ ———

THE NOTED COMMENTATOR, Christian Wolmar, once remarked that 'railways changed the nature of warfare, and created the potential for prolonged and mass warfare'. He went on to say that, 'The difference between fighting wars in the railway era and earlier times was the ability to get very large numbers of men and material quickly to the point where they were needed.'

In fact, the first major military use of the railways was far from home, in the Crimean War, when an 8-mile line between the port of Balaklava and the fort of Sebastopol was built in early 1855 to enable men and supplies to be transported to the siege of the town. The siege was eventually broken, thanks to the greater number of shells that could be taken up the hill on the railway.

So by the outbreak of the First World War, government and military leaders were well aware of the critical importance the railways could play when war was declared and took steps to bring them under government control straightaway. The railway companies were exhausted by the war effort and, by 1923, they re-formed into just four large organisations. A similar pattern was to follow in the 1940s, where

nationalisation followed just three years after the cessation of hostilities.

It is difficult from this distance to imagine the scale of activities on the wartime railways. Prior to the outbreak of the Second World War, the railways were at the peak of their efficiency. In the July and August holiday weeks of 1939 many millions of holidaymakers were taken by train to the seaside and the railways were working flat out 24 hours a day.

Before hostilities started in earnest, the first task of the railways was to help in the evacuation of children from major cities, including those of Liverpool and Manchester, to places of safety. This was carried out with clockwork precision. Eventually, a total of 700 children were to see out the Second World War billeted with well-meaning strangers in Wigan, 500 in Bury, 200 in Oldham and 240 in Rochdale, with many others dotted around more rural parts of Lancashire. Bernadette Johnson in her essay *And the Children Came to Lancashire* wrote that, 'The children came from all walks of life, whilst many were intelligent and well dressed, others were in a deplorable state. They were filthy, their clothing was absolutely disgusting and many were riddled with disease, as if they had stepped straight out of *Oliver Twist*.'

Despite official warnings and widespread publicity of the railways' slogan, 'Is your journey really necessary?', passenger traffic remained very heavy. Before the war, passenger journeys represented 20,000 million miles of travel, and freight traffic 17,000 million ton miles, apart from livestock and the huge quantity of parcels, milk, mail and luggage carried by passenger trains. In 1942 passenger traffic increased, compared with pre-war conditions, by a further

■ *Staff posing in front of a Lancashire & Yorkshire Railway ambulance train in the First World War.* (Author's collection) ■

10,000 million passenger miles, and freight traffic by a further 7,000 million ton miles. The principle adopted for transport in wartime was that the needs of the war must always come first, so absolute priority had to be given to Service movements and then to workers so that they could travel to and from the factories. The large-scale movements of men, materials and munitions presented a huge logistical problem. Many carriages which lacked the comfort of those built in later years had to be pressed into service. Locomotives which used to pull fast passenger trains now hauled troop trains and war freights, whilst several hundred passenger train carriages were converted into carriages for ambulance trains.

The scale of wartime operations dwarfs any comparable peacetime activities. No fewer than 160,000 special trains ran nationally for the conveyance of troops and their equipment between 1939 and 1945. Running trains in the 'blackout' was itself a tricky business: stations could be difficult to spot, especially as their name-boards had been removed; coach windows had to have their blinds down; and locomotives were required to have blackout sheets fitted, held in place by thick rubber bands. Troop specials were additional to the hundreds of thousands of trains operated for the movement of passengers, coal, foodstuffs and supplies of every kind. Much had to be done secretly and at very short notice, ideally with as few people as possible knowing details of what was running and why. Each train that ran on the railway and was not a regular service had to be given a reporting number which it carried on the front of the engine.

This is the story of one such train. Intimation is received at 'Traffic Headquarters', by despatch rider or by telephone, that

27 officers, 390 other ranks, together with 10 tons of equipment, must be moved from Chorley to Portsmouth, and that the train must reach its destination by 6 am on the day after tomorrow. The journey will take the train over portions of the line belonging to three of the four main line railways. The railway on whose territory the train starts is known as the 'initiating' company; that company will sort things until all the arrangements have been made and the train is handed over to the next railway to deal with. The railway on whose line the destination station is located is known as the 'receiving' company.

Though our 'Troop Special' will not be allocated its number for some hours yet, the railway traffic operating experts get busy the moment the request is received. Before it can receive a reporting number, before it really exists as a train, much has to be done. In the course of her journey through Britain, the train will be handed over from one company to another at specified junctions at specified times. The first action was for the initiating company to find out from the two other railways over whose lines the train will travel, at what time they want it to arrive at these specified junctions in order that it may reach Portsmouth at 6 am on the following day.

Having received this information, the work of plotting a 'path' can begin. Perversely, where the arrival time is of major importance, the run is worked out backwards and, actually, the starting time will be the last thing to be determined. The journey is a long one, and the troops will need food en route, so that halts must be planned at places where facilities are available.

The unit can now be told, via the military transport

authorities, that a train will leave Chorley at 12.10 pm, that halts for refreshments will be made at 4 pm. and 8 pm, and that the train will reach Portsmouth at 6 am the next day. At this stage, arrangements can be made in detail for the running and, as many hours as possible prior to the actual running of the train, all these details are confirmed in circulars known as special train notices. By these circulars, control offices, station masters and signalmen on the line of the route are advised of the arrangements for running the train so far as it affects them. Only a very few railway operating officials ever get to know the true character of these trains and their destinations. To the majority of the staff concerned with her running, she will be just one of hundreds of special trains passing along the local railway tracks every day.

Although trains, stations and tracks were an obvious target for enemy air raids, Lancashire's main lines avoided much of the damage found elsewhere. One notable exception was the station in Bootle,

■ *Bomb damage at Bootle caused the closure of the railway station for two years.* (Author's collection) ■

now known as New Strand but which, prior to 1967, was titled Marsh Street and Strand Road. It suffered a direct hit from enemy action aimed at Liverpool's docks on 19th May 1941 and remained closed for over two years, until 12th July 1943. Another attack destroyed a length of track south of Rawtenstall, close to what is now Irwell Vale station.

Generally, though, the railways maintained the capacity to repair bomb damage and be up and running again in an amazingly short period of time. Engineers had designed standard 'universal' bridge spans and other repair materials; and additional steam breakdown cranes were on call and ready to be used on any route whenever required.

So what was Lancashire's particular role in all this extra effort? As described above, several busy mainline railways carried troops, ammunition and all kinds of stock through the county, but here we will concentrate on two particular roles, the manufacture of ordnance and the use of hospitals to care for injured and recovering troops.

The Royal Ordnance factory at Euxton, near Chorley, known as ROF Chorley, was opened in the late 1930s as part of what had been a conscious preparation for renewed hostilities. As built, the site was large enough, covering 928 acres with 1,500 buildings, 25 miles of railway sidings and 50 miles of road surfaces. It was also part of a deliberate policy to disperse armaments and munitions production away from major cities and the south-east of England which were felt to be especially vulnerable to bombing from the air. As a result the Ministry of Supply built a number of Royal Ordnance factories and satellite factories, including the one at Euxton, near Chorley, but even before they were finished it was

realised that they would not have the necessary capacity to meet Britain's need for ammunition. In all, some twenty Government-owned ammunition factories were built during the Second World War, but none was as large or employed as many people as the ones at ROF Chorley and ROF Bridgend in South Wales.

The new factory at Chorley employed over 1,000 production workers by the outbreak of war in September 1939. By June 1940, the numbers employed there had risen to nearly 15,000. At its wartime peak, ROF Chorley had over 28,000 employees – a staggering figure at a time when there were only around a dozen factories in the whole of Britain with a workforce each of more than 19,000 people. ROF Chorley was the site where the bouncing bombs, designed by Barnes Wallis and famed for the 'dambusters' raid, were filled with explosives.

At the peak of the war effort, 7,000 additional trains were being run every week just to convey workers to and from Government factories. At one factory alone nearly a quarter of a million train journeys were being made by workers in over 400 trains every week. Millions of people also worked at privately-owned factories on war work. These were carried by the railways' ordinary train services, augmented as necessary. During 1942, 400 million passenger journeys were made by the holders of Workmen's Tickets, an increase over 1941 of 75 million.

ROF Chorley had its own private railway station, ROF Halt, which continued in use after the war and was last used on 27th September 1965. The railway line, particularly the station, was separated from the ROF by brick boundary walls some

■ *Filling shells at ROF Chorley during the Second World War.* (Bertram Baxter Collection) ■

■ *The site of the former railway state at ROF Chorley. (Author)* ■

20 ft high along each side. Access to the site from the railway station was also by means of an over bridge. The railway station and platforms were demolished in 2002 as the former ROF site was systematically flattened for conversion into housing. The new Buckshaw Parkway railway station, which opened on 3rd October 2011, is built close to, but not quite on, the same site as the old station.

Until the mid 1990s, in the interests of security, Ordnance Survey maps always omitted the ROF sites and any internal railways, instead showing the locations as they existed before the ROF's construction. More recent editions of the maps do show the detail of the buildings, road and rail links, but are labelled simply as 'works'.

During the slack period between 1945 and the Korean war, ROF Chorley, together with a smaller unit at Bridgwater in Somerset, manufactured the concrete components for Airey's two-storey, pre-fabricated concrete houses. Airey houses were made up of concrete planks placed one above the other and are now generally being knocked down and rebuilt as they are not habitable, partly due to asbestos, though it is possible that a few survive in or around Preston. ROF Chorley also manufactured concrete railway sleepers, gate posts and similar structures.

Railways were clearly an important factor in the construction and extension of these new factories and sites.

■ *A surviving traditional signal box at Diggle, on the LNWR's Trans-Pennine route.* (Author) ■

Bricks and building supplies were conveyed as fast as they could be absorbed. Sidings were laid in fields, signal boxes built, new factory stations erected and services arranged both inside and outside the factory areas. Some of the factories were served by main lines, others, some miles from the nearest towns, were linked by specially-built spur lines. One very little known example is that of exchange sidings, mainly for wartime use, which existed south of the village of Brinscall, halfway between Chorley and Blackburn. A short spur off the former LNWR and LYR 'joint line' between the two towns had led to what was known as Brinscall Printworks until this closed in 1928. However, unbeknown to the rest of the world, the system of sidings was enlarged rather than torn up, and was apparently used to store perishable items such as sugar in a location well away from enemy lines. The site of the junction with the former main line, its gates long gone but still marked by concrete posts, may still be identified by those who know where to look. The break-up of industry into dispersed units for strategic reasons meant that instead of carrying materials, goods and workers in bulk to large centres, the railways had to cater for smaller consignments to many varied destinations.

Just a mile or so south of the above site could and, indeed, can still be found one of the county's most secret installations. An ordnance factory was built in Heapey during the Second World War which became part of BAe Systems and had an 'ammunitions storage facility' with some connections to ROF Chorley. Public accounts of this site are very limited but one describes a somewhat frustrating visit, 'Arriving in Heapey I was met by two guys, one in uniform and the other not. No photography was to be permitted. I was shown to the first of four large shutter doors which were built into the hillside and which could just be seen from the adjoining road. Inside were another three sets of doors. I asked the guy in uniform if he would open these as well, but he didn't have the keys. I was told that the space inside was as big as the Reebok Stadium, though divided into compartments, but I never got to see for myself.' When the main ROF factory was in use it probably

■ *A faded notice still visible at the Heapey factory.* (Author) ■

made sense to store the assembled bombs here away from the main factory. The area is still kept secure; the most likely explanation is that the place is probably just used as a storage depot by BAe Systems (BAe Warton is fairly close by).

Lancashire was also home to a number of what where originally known as 'county lunatic asylums' but which became temporary homes to wounded or shell-shocked troops. Three of these institutions had their own rail connections: at Whittingham, near Preston, Calderstones near Clitheroe and Winwick near Warrington.

Originally built as an asylum to house 'idiot boys' in 1896, the Lord Derby War Hospital, situated on the Winwick Rectory Estate, north of Warrington, was used as a military hospital, with 2,160 beds, during both world wars. Between

1915 and 1920 over 56,000 wounded soldiers were treated there, and the hospital resumed its work as an asylum in 1921. A branch line, but perhaps more fairly described as a long siding, reached the hospital site via a junction half a mile or so north of Winwick Quay, delivering coal and other essential goods.

By the time of the First World War, a proper procedure was in place for the return and care of those injured in combat. Trains were also provided for the evacuation of civilian casualties from first aid or clearing stations to hospitals. The sick and wounded were unloaded from hospital ships in Southampton onto designated ambulance trains. These ambulance trains were fully equipped with furnished cars for nurses and doctors, kitchens, wards for stretcher, sitting-up and mental cases, and cars for infectious cases and for travelling pharmacies. Coaching stock from the London & North Western Railway was used for the majority of what became 29 ambulance trains nationally, but of these, seven were actually operated by the Lancashire & Yorkshire Railway.

Let us imagine we are tracking the journey of one of the many ambulance trains that made its way during the First World War to what was known for the duration as Queen Mary's Military Hospital, rather than its peacetime name of Calderstones. For security reasons, strict secrecy was maintained regarding special workings and other arrangements for the smooth transport of the sick and wounded by these hospitals on wheels. Once the train had been loaded with patients at the dockside, a telegram would be sent to Whalley alerting them to the forthcoming arrival of hundreds of men. Although the ambulance trains crossed the whole country, it was still the practice to change engines and crew whenever boundaries were crossed to ensure drivers and firemen were familiar with the route.

To reach Calderstones, the trains would leave the Blackburn to Hellifield line at Barrow Sidings, a mile or so north of Whalley station, and then be slowly propelled up the branch to the hospital. The original layout had left too sharp a change in direction for main line engines, so a second alignment was provided in 1915, with a larger radius curve, and these two parallel formations, in gentle cuttings, may still be viewed. The whistle of the engine on the main line could be heard at the hospital, so medical officers and stretcher bearers would have time to get into position at a makeshift temporary platform ready for the train's arrival. The walking wounded would be the first to disembark, followed by those in wheelchairs and finally those needed to be carried by stretcher.

Whittingham Hospital was, in peacetime, the busiest of these three hospital railways. It had its own station with a covered canopy and, remarkably, offered a service, free of charge, for all who needed to use it from the junction station at Grimsargh until it closed in June 1957.

By the time of the Second World War, the wounded were again transported from ports in ambulance trains to hastily established military hospitals, again in space vacated by large institutions. However, there is no record of such trains travelling up the branches, or sidings, to Winwick, Calderstones or Whittingham – instead their passengers were unloaded at the nearest station, then taken by road ambulance into the hospital itself.

DECLINE AND FALL

∎

TRACING THE START OF THE DECLINE of Britain's railways is not a straightforward task. As we have already seen, Rossendale's quarry traffic was falling away by the end of the Great War, but the demand for coal continued to increase year on year into the 1960s, as did heavy industry such as steelworks and car production.

Passenger traffic reached its peak in the 1920s but figures declined considerably in the 1930s, when car ownership was still minimal. The reason for this drop was almost always bus competition. Buses could collect passengers from village centres, when the railway station was perhaps a mile or so away, and run direct to the market square of the nearest town. With little traffic on the roads then, they could also reliably compete with the railway for speed, too. In places where dormitory suburbs were being built, the railway did fight back by opening new stations in places such as Squires Gate (Blackpool) in 1931, Besses o' th' Barn (Bury) in 1933 and Bowker Vale (North Manchester) in 1937.

Three Lancashire lines lost to passengers at that time, which illustrate the decline very well, include the Garstang & Knott End Railway that opened to Pilling in 1870. After many trials

and tribulations, it eventually reached Knott End by July 1908. Garstang's original station was inconveniently situated almost two miles to the south of the town. As a result, the place and, perhaps more importantly, its market, never developed to any extent and people preferred to travel either south to Preston or north to Lancaster. To the west of Garstang was what was once described as 'a wide expanse of desolate moss' and, despite some efforts to cultivate it, it remains one of Lancashire's least populous areas. So the potential for passenger traffic was severely limited: firstly, numbers were few and, secondly, the railway wasn't taking them directly to the places they wanted to go. A bus could travel from Blackpool to Preston, serving the outlying communities much more conveniently and so, on 5th July 1930, passenger services were finally withdrawn. Two days later a similar fate awaited the Glasson Dock branch, not far to the north. Although trains did go directly to Lancaster, the nearest place of any size, Glasson Dock was, and indeed still is, a tiny community that can easily be served by one small, single-deck omnibus.

The Longridge branch from Preston is a slightly different case, not least because if it was running today it would most likely be very busy and well patronised. This line opened in 1848, with the original intention to extend north-east to Clitheroe. This section was never completed but work did take place at Hurst Green where a cutting, which may still be seen, was constructed that never saw rails or sleepers. Although it also served Ribbleton in Preston's northern suburbs and the village of Grimsargh, the junction for the Whittingham Hospital Branch, it ran almost parallel to the main road and fell victim to a price war with the local bus company. The LMS

■ *A 1960s' view of Carnforth shed.* (Author'collection) ■

■ *A 2008 view inside Manchester Mayfield, Manchester's 'Forgotten Station'. (Author)* ■

as 'common carriers' and therefore obliged to transport everything offered to them until 1962 – only after that time did local stations lose their role as purveyors of small-scale freight traffic.

With the onset of war, followed by years of austerity and fuel rationing, the railway was considered a valuable resource but, by around 1950, it became clear to the newly-nationalised transport authorities that some lines were never going to pay their way. The Bacup to Rochdale line (another that might be very well patronised if still here today) was closed in June 1947, originally as a temporary measure due to fuel shortages, but made permanent in 1949. Other early to mid 1950s' closures included the routes from Rainford

gave up the fight quickly, withdrawing passenger services in June 1930.

All three of these lines did stay open for goods traffic for many years afterwards. Glasson Dock, and to a lesser extent Knott End, had maritime traffic, whilst above Longridge were busy quarries, as well as hospital traffic from Whittingham. But general goods traffic was in decline too, with lorries able to deliver small quantities door to door. Railways were classed

Junction to St Helens and Ormskirk, as well as the short branch to Delph, near Oldham. Both routes from Wigan to Chorley, via Boars Head and via Hindley and Blackrod, followed in 1960 as did the Chorley to Blackburn line.

So, a steady programme of cutting 'unprofitable routes' existed long before the arrival on the scene of Dr Beeching who, to this day, is often wrongly blamed for some closures that look place years before his involvement with the railways.

■ *Hauling freight at Boars Head Junction, north of Wigan. Note the unusual structure of the signal box.* (Glenn Morris) ■

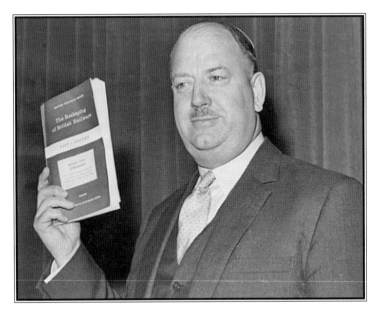

■ *Dr Richard Beeching, chairman of British Railways.*
(Author's collection) ■

The former British Railways chairman, Dr Richard Beeching has long been popularly portrayed as an axe-wielding ogre who closed as many railways as he could, got rid of the universally-loved steam engines and left communities all over Britain with no access to trains. Many people still hold the view that if the dreaded doctor had not descended on the nation's railways in the 1960s, many of the closed lines would still be running today. Still more railway analysts have seriously questioned the criteria used by him and those that came afterwards to justify the closure of individual routes, particularly those serving large centres of population. Coming into the sector from a purely business point of view, in 1963 he produced a report, *The Reshaping of British Railways*, which became one of the seminal documents of British railway history. It led to the closure of around a third of the nation's railway network and a higher proportion of its stations.

Some perspective is needed here. After the austerity of the 1950s, the 1960s was a period of growth, prosperity and all kinds of new freedoms. It was a time when past glories and practices were less valued than they had ever been before or since, and the railways were very much seen as old-fashioned, declining, outdated, dirty, and to be used only by those who could not avail themselves of a nice, shiny, new motor car. The first stretch of motorway in Britain had been built around Preston in 1957 and with Ernest Marples in charge with his dual role as road-builder and Minister for Transport, the trend was clearly in one direction. By 1961 airlines were also competing with the railways. That year, British European Airways introduced their 'Vanguard' service between London and Manchester, significantly beating the railway on price as well as on speed, having already successfully started a similar service to Edinburgh.

Hindsight is, of course, a wonderful thing and the view that Beeching was wrong in this or that case, that route closures were premature and if only the powers that be had foreseen the expansion of rural communities in commuter belt country, and the increase in road congestion from the 1980s onwards, needs to be seen in that context. In fact, it can be argued that the most damaging closures occurred after Beeching, with the

Midland main line from Manchester to the East Midlands via Bakewell closing in 1967 and major towns the size of Leigh and Fleetwood losing their rail services in 1969 and 1970 respectively.

Alongside the decline and fall of the lines and stations was that of the steam locomotive itself. Steam had been gradually pushed out of passenger haulage by electric services and diesel multiple units. Arguments have raged ever since about whether the end of steam was necessary. To many observers it had the smell of a political fix. British Rail had invented InterCity and painted all its carriages blue and white in an early attempt at a corporate image. Steam engines had no place in this vision; they were too obviously mechanical and emitted embarrassing noises and smells. By 1958 a re-appraisal by the British Transport Commission had resulted in a decision to accelerate the disposal of the steam fleet, despite the fact that many of the BR Standard Class 9F 2-10-0s had yet to be built. This course of action was as much related to staffing levels as to the actual efficiencies of the engines themselves – steam needed a driver and a fireman, a constantly topped-up water supply, cleaners and hordes of maintenance staff; a diesel multiple unit needed just a driver and somewhere for it to be serviced at intervals. It takes hours to fire up a steam engine before you can use it but you can get a diesel engine running in less than a minute.

Soon large groups of condemned locomotives were arriving at the major BR works for cutting up and frequently the yards at the works could not cope with storage of such an enormous quantity of engines. Consequently, dumps of withdrawn locomotives began to appear in adjacent sidings or on nearby closed branch lines. Within a very short time, the rate of withdrawals was outstripping the capacity of the main works to dispose of them. Yet some of the steamers were barely ten years old (the last was built in 1960), and they could most probably have lasted another 50 years.

But steam was to survive until the bitter end in Lancashire, until August 1968. Three Lancashire sheds, Carnforth, Lostock Hall near Preston, and Rose Grove near Burnley were the last left open. As at that time Sunday freight traffic was almost non-existent, Sunday, 4th August 1968 was a far from active day at all three depots, being particularly quiet at Carnforth and Rose Grove. All the glory of the occasion, on such an auspicious day, obviously centred upon the various 'Farewell to Steam' specials; indeed, there had probably never been before nor since such a concentration of workings of this nature in a single area, since there were no fewer than six steam-hauled trains planned to be touring Lancashire at the same time. Footplate crews arriving to sign on duty shortly after dawn found the place already a hive of activity, with numerous engines being prepared to work various stages of the aforementioned specials. Official railway personnel on duty proved to be totally outnumbered, both by enthusiasts and other members of the public merely wanting to witness the passing of an era.

Later, there was the somewhat controversial '15-Guinea Special', powered from Merseyside to Carlisle on 14th August by the one remaining Britannia, 70013 *Oliver Cromwell*. The charge was £15.75 – equal to about two weeks' wages then – for the privilege of travelling on the 'last ever' officially-operated steam train. British Railways certainly decided to

■ *Rose Grove Shed, near Burnley.* (Glenn Morris) ■

milk steam buffs for their last penny and there was no shortage of takers. Probably the thousands of people who stood at the line side and watched it go by had a better view. It may have been only a few seconds, but it was more dignified than being on the train, fighting with hundreds of other enthusiasts for a space at one of the tiny windows. Rusty,

neglected engines peered out of the doors of the sheds for the last time. That evening, the very last job undertaken by a steam engine on British Railways was completed at Carnforth. The final fires were allowed to drop that evening. And so ended the steam era in Britain. But as one story ended, another was about to start.

KEEPING STEAM ALIVE

■

NOT FAR FROM CARNFORTH railway station is what used to be the Carnforth Motive Power Depot where many steam engines were based in steam's heyday. Over many years it was known as 'Steamtown' a popular destination for enthusiasts, but no longer. For health and safety reasons, perhaps understandably in this case, in 1997, Steamtown had to stop allowing access to the paying public; they couldn't risk visitors slipping on leaking oil or crashing head first into an inspection pit.

The former Steamtown sheds are now home to the West Coast Railway Company. This firm operates charter trains throughout the year, many of which are hauled by steam locomotives. It has grown to become the UK's leading operator of special trains. The company now provides most of the stock and crews for steam workings on the national network, plus a large amount for diesel tours as well. The headquarters and large engineering base allows space for a wide range of locomotives and stock to be stored, including two former LMS 4-6-0s, one a 'Black Five' and the aforementioned ex-British Railways 4-6-2 'Britannia' *Oliver Cromwell*.

Carnforth is also famous as the location for one of the smokiest and best of railway films, *Brief Encounter* (though the story was set in the Home Counties) which is still played continuously in the visitor centre at the once almost derelict station. It looks uncannily as it did when the movie was first released nearly 60 years ago: the table at which Celia Johnson and Trevor Howard first drank tea together, the wall lights, the till, even the bar-top bottle opener. And there, too, a few feet from the mainline trains that still thunder by, is the door from which Johnson, torn by a doomed and frustrated love, ran out in an apparent suicide attempt.

So authentic is the refurbishment of the most famous railway refreshment room in Britain that an elderly visitor once burst into tears, saying 'This is exactly the way I remember it. This is where I passed by with my friend on my way to war. We had tea and a sandwich here. I came home after the war, he didn't.' It's hard to believe now that such a tale of passion was possible and believable, so much passion, betrayal and suppressed eroticism, the whisper of steam and the gathering thunder of expresses with that final tearful farewell.

After the mainline system had finished, steam addicts could still get their 'fix' but sometimes had to go to the most unlikely places. Working industrial steam lingered on for many years, particularly for shunting coal wagons at collieries. On odd occasions, word got around of forthcoming activity. A steam buff from that era recalled, 'When those occasions arrived, we moved fast. As they became rarer, the pre-internet grapevine kept linesiders informed as to where steam survivors could be found at work. Phones would ring, days off would be taken

■ *Carnforth's station clock seen in the film,* Brief Encounter.
(Author) ■

and photographers would gather to shoot the invariably grubby, leaky engines as they went about their shunting.' The National Coal Board was the most likely operator of the last handful of iron horses, such as at Bold Colliery, near St Helens. One enthusiast recalled 'My phone rang late one evening and a voice said: "There's an 'Austerity' shunting at Bold tomorrow. Let's meet there at 0600 so we can photograph the morning shift. Any shunting needed will be done by 1000." It was freezing and there was snow on the ground. In the shed door an 'Austerity' was brewing, dark coal smoke curling from its chimney and filling the air with that characteristic pungent aroma. It was an entirely unofficial visit. Bright orange NCB boiler suits and white hard hats were found for us, so we blended in somewhat, and we wandered quietly and unobtrusively around the colliery. It was, quite simply, a magical morning.'

The very last such haunt was almost certainly Bickershaw, near Leigh. Bickershaw Colliery opened in 1877 but later was much expanded and deepened to exploit the rich seams beneath until it was linked up to Golborne and Parsonage collieries underground, in a £3 million scheme, completed in 1976. Some 90% of its output was destined for power generation and in 1970 a scheme was devised to divert much of its output to the nearby Fiddlers Ferry power station, which was then being served by coal trains from Yorkshire that travelled across via the now closed Woodhead route. Bickershaw Colliery was connected to a branch line that ran between Platt Bridge and Hindley Green, near Wigan. As BR locos were not allowed on the NCB, the wagons had to be taken by a colliery loco to the bunkers. The colliery was still steam worked well into the 1980s, with a fleet of 0-6-0 Saddle Tank 'Austerity' engines and though a diesel shunter eventually appeared, at least one of the saddle tanks was kept in reserve and may have steamed on odd occasions as late as 1990.

Another great local steam event was the 150th anniversary re-enactment of the Rainhill trials in 1980. The official programme started with a message from Sir Peter Parker, then chairman of the British Railways Board, welcoming visitors to Rainhill and emphasising the importance of the Liverpool and Manchester Railway. It explained that the replicas of the *Rocket*, the *Sans Pareil* and the *Novelty* would pull three replica coaches with passengers on board and would run a course, starting at intervals. On each day, the winning locomotive was to be the one that completed the course quickest, with the engine achieving the quickest aggregate time over the three days being the overall winner. The programme explained, 'We feel the test offers a reasonable challenge to the locomotives, their builders and handlers without in any way

■ *An early 20th-century picture of Fidlers Ferry & Penketh station, Warrington, which closed in 1950. Only the station house survives at the site.* (Author's collection) ■

becoming too serious or attempting to overturn history! We certainly do not hold out any hope that the winner will henceforth be used to work trains on the line!', a subtle reference to the abolition of steam traction on BR.

BY KIND PERMISSION OF BRITISH RAILWAYS

VIEW THE
BRITISH RAIL
RAINHILL TRIALS
SPECTACULAR

from

Rainhill Cricket Club Ground

on

24, 25, 26 MAY, 1980

Southside Grandstand Seat

Tickets £7.50 each

Crossed cheque with S.A.E. to:

The Trials Secretary, Arran, Norlands Lane, Rainhill, Merseyside.

Printed by Leeman Seal House, Neston, South Wirral

■ *A poster for the 150th anniversary re-enactment of the Rainhill Trials. (Author's collection)* ■

Unfortunately, the star of the show *Rocket* derailed three times so never made it to the cavalcade itself. *Novelty* failed to raise sufficient steam and was conveyed on a low-loader wagon. *Sans Pareil* was towed on the westbound journey by a Class 08 shunter but able to return eastbound unassisted. So the wrong engine won the re-enactment of the 1829 trials! BR Chairman Sir Peter Parker and then Minister for Transport, Norman Fowler, should have been conveyed by *Rocket* in an L&M replica coach but instead arrived in a train of three ex-LNWR royal coaches. A problem the organisers had was that since the event was staged on the then – and soon to be again – main line route between Liverpool and Manchester (though now electrified) a test run could not be run prior to the event.

Perhaps the most unlikely venues for the post–1968 enthusiast looking for a breath of smoky air are the miniature seaside railways. Opened in 1911 and having therefore just celebrated its centenary is perhaps one of the best known of such lines: the Lakeside miniature (15 in gauge) railway in Southport. The two tiny 4-4-2 locomotives named *King George* and *Princess Elizabeth* were mainstays of this line, though they were little used after 1970. They were kept in store at Steamtown but returned for one weekend in March 1983 before being eventually exported to the United States. Also of note was a locomotive modelled on the 'A4' streamlined Pacific class but with a diesel-electric engine. The line at Blackpool Pleasure beach is of slightly larger dimensions (20 or 21 ins gauge, sources vary) but has generally used diesel operated models of famous steam locomotives such as the *Flying Scotsman*.

■ *Miniature railways are a popular tourist attraction all over the country.* (Author's collection) ■

■ *Trainspotters at Manchester Victoria station in the 1950s.* (Glenn Morris) ■

Let us now go on to consider the bread and butter of railway enthusiasm – trainspotting. Academic social historians have spent much time trying, with little apparent success, to understand how a mass participation hobby of the 1940s, '50s and '60s managed to acquire the uniquely uncool reputation it has enjoyed in recent times. Perhaps it is simply that modern trains don't deserve the attention bestowed on their predecessors.

Traditionally 'invented' by Ian Allen whose locomotive guides sold up to a million copies at the peak of their popularity in the 1950s, train spotting was quite simply the national hobby for boys during the Fifties; it cut right across all social classes. For many lads it was simply what they did – wait for the train, and then underline the number of the train they had spotted in their book, with their pencil – hours of fun! The question most frequently asked nowadays is 'What on earth did you see in trains?' As a small boy, the fascination for trains was handed down by one's peers – an older brother, for example. There were thousands of boys, this author included, whose penchant for collecting engine numbers came from the simple pleasure of collecting things: stamps, coins or cigarette cards. But, for many, the end of steam overshadowed everything. A spotter and veteran of many trips to Preston, Lancaster (Castle) and Wigan recalled that 'We'd had years to get ready for it, but the 1968 Ian Allan 'combine' still came as a shock. It was so thin and insignificant. But in the four years I'd been buying the 'combine', it had shed thousands of numbers. They'd already stopped issuing a separate steam book – it would have been derisory; no more than a flimsy pamphlet.'

Trainspotter Michael Harvey described a rather dispiriting visit to Lancashire just a few months before the end of steam: 'At Rose Grove we saw 29 locomotives "on shed" and the remains of locomotives that had already been cut up; 8F 2-8-0 No 48544 appeared next in line for the torch. We went on to Lostock Hall where about sixteen engines were dumped in sidings waiting to be towed away for disposal.' Today, countless thousands of ex-spotters still bear the emotional scars of abandoning their allegiance to steam during the 1960s. Other areas battled on with diesels such as 'Westerns' and 'Deltics' to enjoy for a while, but the West Coast Main Line was soon to be electrified and even less affection was bestowed on these anonymous electric locomotives. Many gave up the hobby after that bitter finale came in August 1968, when just five steam locomotives were left: three Black 5s, Nos 44781, 44871, 45110; a solitary 8F No 48448 and the last working 'Britannia' No 70013 *Oliver Cromwell*. Such memories, of course, bring back all sorts of other recollections from that era: Dinky toys, Hornby Dublo trains, Vespa scooters and even Spangles sweets and Tizer or Corona pop to help wash them down.

STILL WITH US

■

THE EAST LANCASHIRE RAILWAY, running these days on an 'L'-shaped route from Rawtenstall to Heywood via Bury, is one of the country's top preserved lines, attracting a wide variety of visitors both on legs and on flanged wheels to the area, indeed perhaps the area's most well-known tourist attraction. What is less well known is that the original plan was to operate on a different piece of track altogether. In the late 1960s, the East Lancashire Railway Preservation Society leased the derelict station site at Helmshore, between Ramsbottom and Accrington, together with a short length of track, to which they moved some steam and diesel locomotives and rolling stock, including guards vans.

After the society had operated its locomotives at this site for a period, it became clear that the railway between Bury, Ramsbottom and Rawtenstall might became available, following the cessation by British Railways of passenger services on 5th June 1972. This length of line was judged to have more potential for the operation of regular steam train services, and the society therefore moved its operational base to Bury. The line at Helmshore was subsequently lifted, with the station being demolished and built over, though the signal box survives in a modified form, having been converted to a small and rather unusual dwelling house.

After British Rail ran the last coal train to Rawtenstall in 1982, it took the East Lancashire Railway five years to prepare the line for passenger use; the line being reopened on 25th July 1987. The initial service operated between Bury and Ramsbottom, via Summerseat. In 1991 the service was extended northwards from Ramsbottom to reach Rawtenstall, via Irwell Vale. However, two original stations on the line, closed to passengers by BR in 1972, have not reopened. They are Ewood Bridge & Edenfield and Stubbins, where a derelict platform and subway may still be seen. Rawtenstall is the practical northern limit of the line as the formation on towards Bacup has had a bypass road built over it almost as far as Cloughfold. In September 2003 an eastbound extension from Bury to Heywood was opened. To reach Heywood the extension had to cross over the Manchester Metrolink line to Bury, close to the site of the former Knowsley Street station. This necessitated the construction of a new intersection bridge, with steeply-graded approaches of 1 in 36 and 1 in 41 nicknamed 'The Ski Jump'. The remainder of the extension includes a long section at 1 in 85, rising towards Heywood, as the line climbs out of the Irwell valley.

The Heritage line is now just over 12 miles long and has a main line connection with the national railway network at Castleton, beyond Heywood. Aspirations exist for extending the running line further to Castleton where an interchange station at Castleton between the East Lancashire Railway and National Rail services might be possible. A rail connection with the Metrolink line also exists, just south of Bury, at Buckley Wells. This was formerly the connection to the Electric Car Shops where the Class 504 EMU sets were maintained, and was created when BR services were diverted to Bury Interchange in 1980. Plans exist to possibly eventually construct and open a station at Buckley Wells, close to the locomotive shed.

The railway is largely run by volunteer members of the East Lancashire Railway Preservation Society (ELRPS). These days it is also well known for its collection of diesel locomotives which reside on the railway, along with over 140 carriages, wagons and utility vehicles. Although the ELR does offer a local residents' discount card, and many residents do use the trains at weekends, it does not claim to offer a true commuter service either in levels of services or fares.

Also well worth a visit is the Ribble Steam Railway, based at Preston Docks. Although never quite on the scale of Liverpool or Heysham, Preston Docks, known as Albert Edward Dock, opened in 1892. At that time it was the largest single dock in the country and, in 1948, it was the first to introduce roll on roll off traffic. This traffic reached a peak in 1968, when 500 dockers were

■ *Ramsbottom station seen from the level crossing gates.* (Author) ■

employed but as the size of ships increased, fewer could use the dock. At the same time, the import of traditional cargoes decreased, and the cost of dredging silt from the channel

■ *The signal box at Ramsbottom. (Author)* ■

increased. In 1979 the decision was made to redevelop the site.

When the final bitumen trains ran in 1995, it looked like the railway's life had come to an end. However, Steamport Southport began negotiations with Preston Borough Council and, during 1999, the group formerly based at the old engine shed in Southport moved to a new home on the dockside at Preston. The steam railway operates weekend return trips on a 1½-mile stretch of trackbed, with a through route used by occasional specials. The Ribble Steam Railway did hope to have a visit in 2012 from the newly-built class A1 locomotive

'Tornado' as part of the Preston Guild celebrations but, unfortunately, this had to be cancelled as it was found that there is a curve on the access line to the RSR that is too tight for Tornado to traverse.

The 2 ft gauge West Lancashire Light Railway (WLLR), near Tarleton, between Southport and Preston, has a surprisingly long history for what appears to be quite a modern operation. The original aim was to save as much as possible of the light railway equipment which was disappearing from those routes that had formerly served local industries. This was some considerable task as it is thought that at one time or another almost a thousand, light, temporary or narrow gauge lines existed in various parts of Lancashire. The first problem was finding a suitable site. This was solved when a strip of land above the clay pits at Alty's Brickworks near Becconsall was purchased. The running line slowly grew in length until it ran from Becconsall to a station known as Asland, which is no longer the far terminus of the line. The line in its present form runs from Becconsall to Delph, with the original track to Asland running on from that station and now used as a storage line. The railway's headquarters and sheds are also situated at Becconsall. What was once just one workshop has been much added to over the years and the equipment allows most of the work on restoring a steam locomotive to be undertaken here, excluding boiler construction.

The WLLR is open to the public on most Sundays and Bank Holidays and passengers can ride in semi-open coaches which have been built by the railway's volunteers. Special weekends are organised, when visiting steam locomotives can also be

■ *Saddle tank,* John Howe, *on the Ribble Steam Railway.* (Author) ■

■ *Arkholme railway station is now a delightful private residence.* (Author's collection) ■

seen in operation and driver, fireman and guard training courses are run for small groups on days when public trains are not operating.

With the aid of television shows and a wide range of books and publications, former railway lines have these days become much more widely recognized as places of recreation, with pleasant and safe routes for pedestrians, cyclists and, in places, horse riders. Old stations such as Arkholme, east of Carnforth (once the home of TV personality and game show host, Jim Bowen) and Delph near Oldham have also been converted into delightful residences.

■ *Delph railway station, near Oldham, another building converted to a private dwelling.* (Author) ■

Official railway paths in Lancashire now exist at a range of locations. These include Ainsdale to Maghull, now forming part of the western end of the Trans Pennine Trail; Accrington to Baxenden; Great Harwood to near Rishton; three routes converging on Lancaster – east to Caton Green, west to Morecambe and south-west to Glasson Dock; Preston to Bamber Bridge along the former East Lancs route, with a return possible on the former horse-drawn Walton Summit Plateway; and on the north side of Preston from Ribbleton towards Grimsargh on the former Longridge branch. However, this is by no means a complete list. Many more unofficial or shorter stretches of under two miles exist such as between Brinscall and Abbey Village (Withnell station) on the Chorley to Blackburn line, several routes around Wigan, the line north of Colne towards Skipton in Yorkshire, and the Delph branch east of Oldham.

Following a formal 'railway path' is not necessarily the only way of exploring old lines, though. Short stretches of trackbed may contain blackberries and other fruit, wild garlic for harvesting and all manner of small wildlife.

Organisations such as the Railway Ramblers Club, (www.railwayramblers.org.uk) which has an active North-West group can arrange walks on privately-owned lines by negotiating with landowners and also explores less well-known lines such as the Rossendale Tramways.

The Accrington route mentioned above has one particularly notable structure. It features a striking causeway across Platts Lodge Lake, starting near Accrington station, which has been built between the piers of the former railway viaduct just a safe distance above the water level of the lake. The piers have been painted a bright red colour, looking rather like a series of giant pillar-boxes stretching across the water.

A recent development has been the opening in 2012 of a replacement viaduct at Woolfold on the former Holcombe Brook branch, north of Bury. This creates a near continuous route for walking and cycling between the River Irwell north of Bury and Greenmount. The new viaduct is a quite spectacular concrete structure, which contrasts nicely with the two original brick-built viaducts elsewhere on the line.

Sometimes there is pleasure to be had just in tracing a long-forgotten route. Let us now imagine that we are looking at a line with the most minimal remains. We have identified the route from an old map, and do not believe that much has been built over. Our next problem is going to be access – is the land owned privately, and if so can you find out by whom? Trespass is a civil (not criminal) offence in England Wales, though damage to property, including crops, might very well be

criminal. So it is a much better idea to identify the landowners and write or phone for permission to enter their land. Having given a good reason, many (but not all) landowners will be happy enough to allow access and might possibly be prepared to assist you with names and contact details for the next landowners up or down the line. But if a landowner says no, you have to respect that, and they don't have to give any reason or justification for their decision. You are most likely to get your first glimpse of the course of the railway where it crosses a road or public right of way. You may first want to know if road and railway were there at the same time, if so there must have been some form of bridge or else a level crossing – but don't go looking for such things if the road was put through long after the railway was closed. Similarly the presence of older houses or other buildings that would have been contemporary to the line can often give a clue to its course.

So much remains to be seen of our steam heritage, both on existing lines and those now closed. Much of it is taken for granted by those who pass by, without any thought to the historical significance, yet an interested layman can develop an eye, an awareness of such things. And there are still surprises, new discoveries to be made. I was delighted to recently discover a whole new system of narrow gauge quarry tramways, hitherto unknown to me, close to Hoghton Tower between Preston and Blackburn. So, I urge you to head out and enjoy Lancashire's railways.

BIBLIOGRAPHY

◼

Ashmore, O., *The Industrial Archaeology of North West England* (Manchester University Press)

Bushell, J., *The World's Oldest Railway* (Crown Press (Keighley)

Careter, O., *An illustrated History of British Railway Hotels* (Silver Link Publishing)

Cornwell M., *The History of the Calderstones Hospital Railway* (self-published)

Cornwell M., *The History of the Whittingham Hospital Railway* (self-published)

Croft, D. J., *A Survey of Seaside Miniature Railways* (Oakwood Press)

Donaghy, T. J., *Liverpool & Manchester Railway Operations 1831–1845* (David & Charles)

Fernyhough, F., *The Liverpool & Manchester Railway 1830–1980* (Robert Hale)

Fletcher, M. & Taylor, J., *Railways – The Pioneer Years* (Studio Editions)

Guy, A. & Rees, J., *Early Railways 1569–1830* (Shire Publications)

Harvey, M.G., *Forget the Anorak – What Trainspotting Was Really Like* (The History Press)

Holt, G. O., *Regional History of the Railways of Great Britain, vol 10 – The North West* (David & Charles)

Huson, S., *Derbyshire in the Age of Steam* (Countryside Books)

Jordan, A. and Jordan E., *Away for the Day – the Railway Excursion in Britain* (Silver Link Publishing)

Jones, M., *Lost Railways of North Wales* (Countryside Books)

Jones, M. A., *Discovering Britain's First Railways – A guide to horse-drawn tramroads and waggonways* (The History Press)

Maggs, C. G., *Bristol & Bath Railways – the Age of Steam* (Countryside Books)

Martin, R., *North West Railway Walks* (Sigma Leisure publishing)

Marshall, J., *Forgotten Railways – North West England* (David & Charles)

Morgan, R., *Railways: Civil Engineering* (Arrow Books)

Mortimer, I., *The Time Traveller's Guide to Medieval England* (Vintage Books)

Pertwee, W., *The Station Now Standing* (Hodder & Stoughton)

Pitt, C., *A Long Time Gone* (Portway Press)

Pixton, R., *Main Line Railways around Wigan* (Runpast Publishing)

Quinn, T., *Tales of the Old Railwaymen* (David & Charles)

Reed, B., *Crewe to Carlisle* (Ian Allan)

Roberts, B., *Railways and Mineral Tramways of Rossendale* (Oakwood Press)

Russell, R., *Lost Canals & Waterways of Britain* (Sphere Books)

Stead, C., *The Birth of the Steam Locomotive – A New History* (Fern House)

Suggitt, G., *Lost Railways of Lancashire* (Countryside Books)

Suggitt, G., *Lost Railways of Merseyside & Greater Manchester* (Countryside Books)

Thomas, D. St John, *The Country Railway* (David & Charles)

Thorpe, D., *The Railways of the Manchester Ship Canal* (Oxford Publishing Company)

Tolson, J. M., *The St Helens Railway* (Oakwood Press)

Townley, C. H. A., Smith, F. D. & Peden, J. A. *The Industrial*

Railways of the Wigan Coalfield Vols 1 & 2 (Runpast Publishing)

Vinter, J., Vinter's *Railway Gazetteer: A Guide to Britain's Old Railways That You Can Walk or Cycle* (The History Press)

Voice, D., *Hospital Tramways and Railways* (Adam Gordon)

Webb, B. & Gordon, D. A., *Lord Carlisle's Railways* (RCTS Publications)

Wells, J., *Railways in and around Bury* (Book Law – Railbus Publications)

ACKNOWLEDGEMENTS

I would like to acknowledge all the help and support I have received in the preparation of this book. Such support has come in many forms. In this regard I would especially like to thank Ian Edwards, Jeff Vinter, Mike Hodgson, Glenn Morris, Brian Slater, Bernard Parkinson, Gordon Suggitt, Leslie Oppitz, Gerald Leach, Phillip Earnshaw, Dave White and the late Ralph Rawlinson. Finally and most importantly, I would like to thank my son Connor, for accompanying me on various trips to far-flung parts of the county and for putting up with my not infrequent absences from my family responsibilities.

INDEX

■